DAILY PRAYER AND PRAISE

THIS book of morning and evening prayers for a month follows a simple pattern. Each morning there is usually:

A prayer of worship, preparation or dedication;

A Bible reading, for which a key verse is printed;

A short meditation on the Bible passage;

A period of silence, so that the Holy Spirit may put into our minds any thought or direction;

A prayer arising from it;

A prayer for the day or some aspect of life;

A prayer for loved ones;

A thought to remember during the day.

Each evening there is:

A section of praise, usually a psalm, recalling the morning meditation;

A prayer of thanksgiving for the day;

A prayer of penitence;

A prayer for the Church;

A prayer of love for those in need;

A last thought of commendation, trust or love.

It is the hope of the editor and the compiler that people who use this book will be able to continue its pattern with their own prayers and in their own words.

DAILY PRAYER
AND
PRAISE

Daily Prayer and Praise was first published in a much shorter version as a part of the series, World Christian Books, sponsored by the Commission of World Mission and Evangelism of the World Council of Churches, and was used as a devotional guide by Christians in many lands. The director of World Christian Books was Stephen Neill, and the editor was John Goodwin. A biographical sketch of George Appleton, author and compiler of this volume, is given at the back of the book.

DAILY PRAYER
AND
PRAISE

compiled by
GEORGE APPLETON

THE WESTMINSTER PRESS
PHILADELPHIA

First published, 1962, by Lutterworth Press
Eighth impression 1972
Revised editions first published 1978

Published by The Westminster Press®
Philadelphia, Pennsylvania

Printed in the United States of America

9 8 7 6 5 4 3 2 1

LIBRARY OF CONGRESS CATALOGING IN PUBLICATION DATA

Appleton, George, Abp.
  Daily prayer and praise.

  Includes index.
  1. Devotional calendars. 2. Prayers. I. Title.
BV4811.A6 1978   242'.2   78-10551
ISBN 0-664-24251-0

Dedicated to the people of St. Botolph, Aldgate,
in gratitude for their friendship and partnership,
1957–1962

CONTENTS

MORNING AND EVENING PRAYERS

I BELONG TO GOD

1 WORSHIP

Blessed be God, the only God: three persons in one eternity of love. Blessed be God for all that he is. Blessed be God for all that he has done, blessed in his church on earth, and blessed in the height of heaven; blessed from everlasting, blessed now, and blessed for evermore. Blessed be God.

BIBLE READING   *Genesis* 1:1, 26, 31

In the beginning God created the heavens and the earth. ... Then God said, Let us make man in our image, after our likeness; and let them have dominion ... over all the earth ... and God saw everything that he had made, and behold, it was very good.

Meditation: God created me: I belong to him. I am a creature of God: I depend on him. I am made in the image of God: I will try to live like Jesus Christ, the perfect image of God. When God seeks me, I will not hide from him; when he speaks I will listen and obey.

SILENCE

Prayer: Grant us, O God, to see beyond the 2
beauty of the earth the glory that is of thee.
Open our eyes to all the signs of thy love.
Enable us so to live that we may hold all created
things in reverence for thy sake who made and
dost sustain them; through Jesus Christ our
Lord.

PRAYER FOR TODAY

O heavenly Father, in whom we live and move 3
and have our being, we humbly pray thee so to
guide and govern us by thy Holy Spirit, that in all
the cares and occupations of our daily life we may
never forget thee, and remember that we are ever
walking in thy sight; through Jesus Christ our
Lord.

PRAYER OF LOVE 4

O Lord our God, from whom neither life nor
death can separate those who trust in thy love, and
whose love holds in its embrace thy children in
this world and the next; so unite us to thyself that
in fellowship with thee we may always be united
to our loved ones whether here or there: give us
courage, constancy and hope; through him who
died and was buried and rose again for us, Jesus
Christ our Lord.

TO REMEMBER TODAY 5

I will sing unto the Lord as long as I live: I will
praise my God while I have my being.

6 PRAISE—FOR CREATION
Almighty God, whose glory the heavens are telling, the earth thy power, and the sea thy might, and whose greatness all thy creatures that think and feel everywhere proclaim: to thee belong all glory, honour, might, greatness, and splendour, now and for ever, world without end.

7 THANKSGIVING FOR TODAY
O God, I thank thee for life and being, and for all the blessings of the past day, for the love that I have received and given, for all the kindnesses that I have received from others and for thy grace going before me and following after me. Above all I thank thee for him through whom I know of thy love and receive thy grace, even Jesus Christ my Lord and Saviour.

8 PENITENCE FOR TODAY
Lord, as I look back over today I realize how often I have forgotten thee and sinned against thee and against thy other children. Let me hear thy voice saying to me, "Child, thy sins are forgiven thee," and let me accept thy forgiveness with a humble and grateful heart, through my Saviour Jesus Christ.

O Lord, who hast set before us the great hope that thy kingdom shall come, and hast taught us to pray for its coming: give us grace to discern the signs of its dawning, and to work for the perfect day when thy will shall be done on earth as it is in heaven; through Jesus Christ our Lord.

EVENING PRAYER 10

O Almighty Father, who in thy divine mercy dost cover the earth with the curtain of darkness, that all the weary may rest; grant unto all men rest in thee this night. Let thy grace comfort and support all who are to spend it in sorrow, in anxiety, or in affliction. We commend into thy hands all our dear relations, friends and neighbours. Strengthen and confirm thy faithful people, convert the wicked, arouse the careless, recover the fallen, relieve the sick, give peace to the dying, guide the perplexed and remove all hindrances to the apprehension of thy truth, that thy holy name may be glorified in Jesus Christ, our Lord and Saviour.

A LAST THOUGHT 11

I will lay me down in peace, and take my rest: for it is thou, Lord, only, that make me dwell in safety.

FATHER! MY FATHER!

12 WORSHIP

We give thee thanks, holy Lord, Father Almighty, eternal God, who hast been pleased to bring us through the night to the hours of morning: we pray thee graciously to grant that we may pass this day without sin, so that at eventide we may again give thanks to thee; through Jesus Christ our Lord.

BIBLE READING   *Galatians* 4:4–6; *Romans* 8:14

But when the time had fully come, God sent forth his Son... that we might receive adoption as sons. And because you are sons, God has sent the Spirit of his Son into our hearts, crying, "Abba! Father!" ...For all who are led by the Spirit of God are sons of God.

Meditation: I am a child of God. So I reverence my Father; I love my Father; I will obey my Father. Not only my Father, but the Father of all who come to him with Jesus Christ. So I am brother to all other Christians. God wills all men to become his children.

SILENCE

Prayer: Almighty God, the Father of our Lord 13
Jesus Christ and our Father, remind us each day
that we are thy children. Help us to live in the
family spirit, knowing that all other people are
called to be thy children also. Help us to repro-
duce the family likeness and to grow day by day
more like thine only begotten Son, Jesus Christ
our Lord.

PRAYER FOR THE KINGDOM 14
I would call down thy blessing today upon all who
are striving for a better world; for all who are
working for juster laws; for all who are working
for peace between the nations; for all who are
engaged in healing divisions and relieving poverty; for all who preach the gospel and for all who
bear witness to Christ in their daily lives. Bless
them and strengthen them to build thy kingdom.

CHRIST WITHIN 15
O my divine Master, teach me to hold myself in
silence before thee, to adore thee in the depths of
my being, to wait upon thee always and never ask
anything of thee but the fulfilment of thy will.
Teach me to let thee act in my soul, and form in it
the simple prayer that says little but includes
everything. Grant me this favour for the glory of
thy name.

TO REMEMBER TODAY 16
I have loved thee, with an everlasting love.

17 *O Father of our Lord Jesus Christ, from whom every family in heaven and on earth is named, grant that according to the riches of thy glory we may be strengthened in the inner man through thy Spirit; that Christ may dwell in our hearts through faith; that we may be rooted and grounded in love.*

18 THANKSGIVING FOR TODAY
Glory be to thee, my God, for all the blessings of the past day; for thy presence ever with me, for the love of family and friends, for every kindness shown me by others, for the satisfaction of my work, and for the knowledge that I am held safe in thy hand whatever happens. I lift my heart in love and gratitude to thee, dear Father, praising thee that thou hast made me thy child through Jesus Christ.

19 CONFESSION FOR TODAY
Father, I have sinned aginst thee and am not worthy to be called thy son. I recall the failures of the day ... and ask thy forgiveness. Let thy Holy Spirit probe into the depths of my heart, cleansing me from all evil, and strengthening my will to desire and do thy will, through thy perfect Son, Jesus Christ my Saviour.

THANKSGIVING FOR THE CHURCH

O eternal Lord God, whose mighty acts have been graciously manifested in the creation of the world and the redemption of mankind, and whose Spirit has called men and women in successive ages to proclaim and extend thy purpose of salvation: accept, we pray thee, our humble thanksgiving for thy blessing upon the church, from its foundation until now, and for the wealth of dedicated lives, converted souls, and healing ministries, which have sprung from its labours; and by the remembrance of these loving kindnesses, strengthen us to pray, to offer and to work for the millions yet awaiting the tidings of thy love and for the triumph of thy everlasting kingdom; through Jesus Christ our Lord.

PRAYER OF LOVE

Watch thou, O Lord, with those who wake, or watch, or weep tonight, and give thine angels charge over those who sleep. Tend thy sick ones, O Lord Christ; rest thy weary ones; bless thy dying ones; soothe thy suffering ones; pity thine afflicted ones; shield thy joyous ones. And all, for thy love's sake.

A LAST PRAYER

Father, into thy hands I commend my spirit, for thou hast redeemed me, O Lord, thou God of truth.

CREATOR SPIRIT

23 WORSHIP

Blessed be the hour, O Christ, in which thou wast born, and the hour in which thou didst die:
Blessed be the dawn of thy rising again, and the high day of thine ascending.
O most merciful and mighty Redeemer Christ, let all times be the time of our presence with thee, and of thy dwelling in us.

BIBLE READING   *Genesis* 1:1–2

In the beginning God created the heavens and the earth. The earth was without form and void, and darkness was upon the face of the deep; and the Spirit of God was moving over the face of the waters.

Meditation: The Holy Spirit moving over the formless earth, bringing order out of chaos, light out of darkness, life from the lifeless. . . . The Holy Spirit moving over my spirit, bringing form, light and life . . . bringing order out of my muddled restless spirit . . . wanting to create something beautiful, something for the glory of God . . . reproducing the image of God in me . . . the likeness of Jesus Christ, Son of God and Son of Man.

Prayer: Trusting in thy word, O Lord, we wait 24
for thy Spirit. Send him forth from thy holy
heaven, to sanctify our hearts, our deeps, which
without him are empty and without form. Give
us grace to remain humble and still under his
action. Quicken us, O Lord, according to thy
lovingkindness.

PRAYER FOR OUR LOVED ONES 25

O God our Father, we bring before thee all those
whom we love, knowing that thou dost love them
more even than we do and that thy will for them is
something better than we can imagine or desire.
Let thy will be done in them and for them, and
grant them that strength which shall make them
more than conquerors, through him who loves
them and us, Jesus Christ our Lord.

THROUGH THY SPIRIT 26

All through this day, O Lord, let me touch the
lives of others for good, by the power of thy
quickening Spirit, whether through the word I
speak, the prayer I breathe, or the life I live. In the
name of Jesus.

TO REMEMBER TODAY 27

Whither shall I go then from thy spirit, or whither
shall I go then from thy presence?

28 PRAISE FOR THE HOLY SPIRIT MOVING OVER US

Whither shall I go then from thy Spirit: or whither shall
* I go then from thy presence?*
If I climb up into heaven, thou art there: if I go down to
* hell, thou art there also.*
If I take the wings of the morning: and remain in the
* uttermost parts of the sea;*
Even there also shall thy hand lead me: and thy right
* hand shall hold me. I will give thanks unto thee, for I*
* am fearfully and wonderfully made: marvellous are*
* thy works, and that my soul knoweth right well.*

29 PRAYER FOR HOLINESS

    O Spirit of God
      who dost speak to spirits
        created in thine own likeness:
    Penetrate into the depths of our spirits,
      into the storehouse of memories
        remembered or forgotten,
    into the very springs of personality,
      and cleanse
        and forgive.

30 THANKSGIVING FOR TODAY

O Lord my God, I thank thee that thou hast been
with me through every minute of this day. I thank
thee that thou hast kept me free from harm and
danger. I thank thee for thy grace in difficulty and
temptation. I thank thee that thy Spirit is ever at

work in me to make me a true child of thine, growing daily in the likeness of thy blessed Son, Jesus Christ, my Lord.

FOR RENEWAL OF THE CHURCH 31

Spirit of promise, Spirit of unity, we thank thee that thou art also the Spirit of renewal. Renew in the whole church, we pray thee, that passionate desire for the coming of thy kingdom which will unite all Christians in one mission to the world. May we all grow up together into him who is our head, the Saviour of the world, and our only Lord and Master.

PRAYER OF LOVE 32

Show thy lovingkindness tonight, O Lord, to all who stand in need of thy help. Be with the weak to make them strong, and with the strong to make them gentle. Cheer the lonely with thy company and the worried with thy peace. Prosper thy church in the fulfilment of her mighty task, and grant thy blessing to all who have toiled today in Christ's name.

A LAST THOUGHT 33

The darkness is no darkness with thee, but the night is as clear as the day: the darkness and light to thee are both alike.

ONE MAN'S OBEDIENCE

34 BEFORE PRAYER

O Holy Spirit, be with us in this time of prayer, and grant us living touch with thee. Give us the insights of thy kingdom, the vision of thy purpose, the guidance of thy wisdom, and grace to be fellow-workers with thee in the doing of thy just and loving will, through Jesus Christ our Lord.

BIBLE READING   *Genesis* 12:1–3

Now the Lord said to Abram, "Go from your country and your kindred and your father's house to the land that I will show you. And I will make of you a great nation, and I will bless you, and make your name great, so that you will be a blessing. I will bless those who bless you, and him who curses you I will curse; and by you all the families of the earth shall bless themselves."

Meditation: God's eternal purpose is to bless all nations. It begins with the response of one man, who goes out in faith not knowing where God will lead him. So Abraham becomes the Father of the faithful. If we are the spiritual descendants of Abraham we must have a similar faith and readiness for adventure.

Prayer: O Lord God, who hast called thy servants to ventures of which we cannot see the ending, by paths as yet untrodden, through perils unknown: Give us faith to go out with a good courage, not knowing whither we go, but only that thy hand is leading us, and thy love supporting us; to the glory of thy name. **35**

FOR FAMILY LIFE
Remember those whom you love, mention them by name, one by one, and hold them in his presence for his blessing. Then pray for all families.

FOR FAMILIES **36**
Almighty Father, from whom every family in heaven and on earth is named: we entreat thy mercy for the families of this and every land, for man and wife and child, and for all who have the care of children; that by thy hallowing our homes may be blessed and our children may grow up in the knowledge of thee and of thy Son, Jesus Christ our Lord.

TO REMEMBER TODAY **37**
Lead me, O Lord, in thy righteousness; make thy way plain before my face.

38 PRAISE FOR GOD'S PURPOSE

God be merciful unto us, and bless us: and show us the light of his countenance and be merciful unto us;

That thy way may be known upon earth: thy saving health among all nations.

O let the nations rejoice and be glad: for thou shalt judge the folk righteously and govern the nations upon earth.

Let the people praise thee, O God: let all the people praise thee.

Then shall the earth bring forth her increase: and God, even our own God, shall give us his blessing.

God shall bless us: and all the ends of the world shall fear him.

39 ACT OF PENITENCE

Almighty God, long-suffering and of great goodness: we confess to thee, we confess with our whole heart: our neglect and forgetfulness of thy commandments: our wrong-doing, speaking and thinking: the hurts we have done to others: and the good we have left undone: O God, forgive thy people that have sinned against thee: and raise us to newness of life.

40 ACT OF GRATITUDE

Almighty God, Father of all mercies, we thine unworthy servants do give thee most humble and hearty thanks for all thy goodness and loving-kindness to us, and to all men; we bless thee for our creation, preservation, and all the blessings of this life; but above all, for thine inestimable love in the redemption of the world by our Lord Jesus Christ, to whom with thee and the Holy Spirit be all honour and glory, world without end.

FOR THE CHURCH WHERE WE WORSHIP 41

O Lord Jesus Christ, who art thyself the temple of the holy city of God, the light thereof and its surpassing glory; glorify and lighten, we beseech thee, with thy perpetual presence this earthly house built gloriously to thee; and be pleased both to inspire and to accept its worship day by day, the praise of thankful lips and the prayers of faithful hearts; who livest and reignest with the Father and the Holy Spirit, one God, for ever and ever.

FOR THE HOMELESS 42

O Christ our Lord, who didst go forth in home-lessness that thou mightest find a home in every man, and that every man might find a home in thee: we bring before thee at this time all thy homeless ones, all who are in exile or in suffering, all refugees; grant them the sense of being held fast in thee, and enable all who love thee to strive together for a world which shall be closer to thy kingdom, in which men may live together as a family, each caring for all, and all caring for each, for the sake of peace.

A LAST THOUGHT 43

Thou wilt keep him in perfect peace, whose mind is stayed on thee; because he trusteth in thee.

NEVER ALONE

44 PRAYER OF DEDICATION
Almighty and eternal God, so draw our hearts to
thee, so guide our minds, so fill our imaginations,
so control our wills, that we may be wholly thine,
utterly dedicated unto thee; and then use us, we
pray thee, as thou wilt, but always to thy glory
and the welfare of thy people, though our Lord
and Saviour, Jesus Christ.

BIBLE READING   *Genesis* 28:10–15
Behold, I am with you and will keep you where-
ever you go, and will bring you back to this land;
for I will not leave you until I have done that of
which I have spoken to you.

Meditation: Jacob, running away from the anger of
his brother, homesick and lonely, finds that God's
presence is still with him. He hears God's promise to
be with him always. Let us take his promise to
ourselves and resolve to remember his presence in
times of temptation, difficulty and loneliness.

SILENCE

Prayer: O God, who art enthroned on high, yet **45** hast thy dwelling-place among the sons of men: Grant that in all the perplexities of life we may see the ladder which stretches from heaven to earth, and the angels of thy presence ascending and descending on it, through Jesus Christ our Lord.

FOR ABSENT FRIENDS **46**

O God, who art everywhere present, look down with thy mercy upon those who are absent from among us. Give thy holy angels charge over them, and grant that they may be kept safe in body, soul and spirit, and be presented faultless before the presence of thy glory with exceeding joy; through Jesus Christ our Lord.

ALL THAT COMES **47**

O Lord, let me not henceforth desire health or life except to spend them for thee and with thee. Thou alone knowest what is good for me; do therefore what seemeth thee best. Give to me or take from me; I desire to adore equally all that comes to me from thee, my Lord and God.

TO REMEMBER TODAY **48**

Behold, I am with you and will keep you where-ever you go.

49 PRAISE

I will lift up mine eyes unto the hills: from whence cometh my help.

My help cometh even from the Lord: who hath made heaven and earth.

The Lord himself is thy keeper: the Lord is thy defence upon thy right hand.

The Lord shall preserve thee from all evil: yea, it is even he that shall keep thy soul.

The Lord shall preserve thy going out, and thy coming in: from this time forth for evermore.

50 PRAYER FOR FORGIVENESS

O Lord Jesus Christ, son of the living God, who at this evening hour didst rest in the sepulchre, and didst thereby sanctify the grave to be a bed of hope to thy people: Make us so to abound in sorrow for our sins which were the cause of thy passion, that when our bodies lie in the dust, our souls may rest with thee; who livest and reignest with the Father and the Holy Spirit, one God, world without end.

51 THANKSGIVING FOR TODAY

O my God, as I come to the end of another day, I lift a grateful heart to thee, I thank thee for thy presence with me, I thank thee for the love of family and friends, for the kindness that I have received today, for the joy of living and for the satisfaction of daily work. I thank thee for thy patience with me, for thy forgiveness and for the grace made available for me through Jesus Christ, thy Son, my Lord.

PRAYER FOR THE CHURCH 52

O Lord, we beseech thee, let thy continual pity cleanse and defend thy church; and, because it cannot continue in safety without thy succour, preserve it evermore by thy help and goodness; through Jesus Christ our Lord.

PRAYER OF LOVE 53

O God of all mercy and love, I bring before thee all in need of thy help tonight—those in sickness and pain, the dying, the lonely and the sad. Grant that they may all look up to thee, to receive that strength which shall make them more than conquerors, through him that loves us all, even Jesus Christ our Saviour.

A LAST PRAYER 54

Preserve us, O Lord, while waking, and guard us while sleeping, that awake we may watch with Christ, and asleep we may rest in peace.

HE WHO IS

55 WORSHIP

O my God, thou thyself art thine own praise; nor canst thou worthily be praised by any other than thyself; for of all things thou art the maker and ruler, and from thee do all things come. Ever therefore shouldst thou be praised and blessed by every creature. May every name that can be used of thee, and every word that can be spoken of thee, praise thee and magnify thee for ever.

BIBLE READING   *Exodus* 3:1–6, 11–14

Then Moses said to God, "If I come to the people of Israel and say to them, 'The God of your fathers has sent me to you,' and they ask me, 'What is his name?' what shall I say to them?" God said to Moses, "I Am who I Am." And he said, "Say this to the people of Israel, 'I Am has sent me to you.'"

Meditation: God is the only being who can say I AM in his own right. Everything else exists because of him. He is the one eternal, the changeless, the great reality from which everything begins, the source of all being, the ground of all existence. My response to his presence must be one of humble dependence, worship and obedience.

Prayer: God is what thought cannot better; God 56
is whom thought cannot reach; God no thinking can even conceive. Without God, men can
have no being, no reason, no knowledge, no
good desire, nought. Thou, O God, Art who
Thou Art, transcending all.

DESIRE FOR GOD   57
Almighty and eternal God,
Thou hast breathed thy Spirit into my spirit;
Thou hast formed my mind to seek thee;
Thou hast inclined my heart to love thee;
Thou hast made me restless for the rest that is in
    thee;
Thou hast planted within me a hunger and a thirst
    that make me dissatisfied with all the joys of
    earth.
O satisfy me with thy mercy and that soon, so
    shall I rejoice and be glad all the days of my life.

FOR OUR HOMES   58
Visit, we beseech thee, O Lord, our homes, and
drive from them all the snares of the enemy; let
thy holy angels dwell in them to preserve us in
peace; and may thy blessing be upon us evermore;
through Jesus Christ our Lord.

TO REMEMBER TODAY   59
Thou art my God, and I will thank thee: Thou art
my God, and I will praise thee.

60 PRAISE—FOR ALL THAT GOD IS

> *O the depth of the riches*
> *and wisdom and knowledge of God!*
> *How unsearchable are his judgments*
> *and how inscrutable his ways!*
> *For who has known the mind of the Lord,*
> *or who has been his counsellor?*
> *Or who has given a gift to him*
> *that he might be repaid?*
> *For from him*
> *and through him*
> *and to him are all things.*
> *To him be glory for ever. Amen.*

61 CONFESSION

Father, Lord of heaven and earth, I confess to thee all the hidden and open sins of my heart and mind, which I have committed unto this day. Wherefore I beg of thee, the merciful and righteous Judge, forgiveness and grace to sin no more, for the sake of Jesus Christ, my Lord and Saviour.

62 AMBASSADORS FOR GOD

O God, who in thy Son Jesus Christ hast reconciled us unto thyself, and hast called us to be ambassadors to the world of that reconciliation: Help us to be reconciled with each other that the world may believe us when we preach the gospel of thy reconciliation in Jesus Christ, the only Mediator and Saviour.

Grant, O Lord, to all those who are bearing pain, thy spirit of healing, thy spirit of peace and hope, of courage and endurance. Cast out from them the spirit of anxiety and fear; grant them perfect confidence and trust in thee, that in thy light they may see light; through Jesus Christ our Lord.

FOR ALL WHO WORK BY NIGHT **64**

Bless, O Lord, all those who, in the night, watch over our lives and homes, and guard all who through the hours of darkness carry on the un-resting commerce of men by land and sea and air. Grant them rest and refreshment, and make us thankful for their service; through Jesus Christ our Lord.

A LAST THOUGHT **65**

This God is our God for ever and ever: He shall be our guide unto death.

FIRST ALWAYS

66 PREPARATION

O thou to whom all hearts are opened, cleanse the thoughts of my heart. O thou to whom all desires are known, strengthen my desire for thee. O thou from whom no secrets are hid, dwell in the very depths of my being, and make me holy. For thy name's sake.

BIBLE READING *Deuteronomy* 6:4–9

Hear, O Israel: The Lord our God is one Lord, and you shall love the Lord your God with all your heart, and with all your soul, and with all your might.

> *Meditation: Jesus picked this out as the first and greatest commandment: to put God first in everything. If we truly love God with all our heart we shall want to do his will. That is the test of our love. His will is the best, the wisest and the most loving thing we can imagine.*

SILENCE

Prayer: O God, who hast prepared for them that 67
love thee such good things as pass man's understanding: Pour into our hearts such love toward
thee, that we, loving thee above all things, may
obtain thy promises, which exceed all that we
can desire; through Jesus Christ our Lord.

WITH MY WHOLE HEART 68
Give me, O Lord, a steadfast heart, which no
unworthy affection may drag downwards; give
me an unconquered heart, which no tribulation
can wear out; give me an upright heart, which no
unworthy purpose may tempt aside. Bestow
upon me also, O Lord my God, understanding to
know thee, diligence to see thee, wisdom to find
thee, and a faithfulness that may finally embrace
thee.

FOR HOMES OF LOVE 69
Lord God Almighty, Father of every family,
against whom no door can be shut: Enter all
homes, we beseech thee, with the angel of thy
presence, to hallow them in pureness and beauty
of love; and by thy dear Son, born in a stable,
move our hearts to hear the cry of the homeless,
and to convert all sordid and bitter dwellings into
households of thine; through Jesus Christ our
Lord.

TO REMEMBER TODAY 70
O my God, I can never love thee enough.

71 PRAISE—FOR GOD'S LOVE
O God, thou art my God: early will I seek thee.
For thy lovingkindness is better than the life itself: my
*   lips shall praise thee.*
As long as I live will I magnify thee on this manner: and
*   lift up my hands in thy name.*
Whom have I in heaven but thee: and there is none upon
*   earth that I desire in comparison of thee.*
My flesh and my heart faileth: but God is the strength of
*   my heart, and my portion for ever.*

72 CONFESSION
O God, our Father, we have sinned against thee in
thought, word, and deed: we have not loved thee
with all our heart; we have not loved our
neighbours as ourselves. Have mercy upon us, we
beseech thee; cleanse us from our sins; and help us
to overcome our faults; through Jesus Christ our
Lord.

73 FOR THE WORK OF THE CHURCH
O Lord, without whom our labour is but lost, and
with whom thy little ones go forth as the mighty;
be present to all works in thy church which are
undertaken according to thy will, and grant to thy
labourers a pure intention, patient faith, sufficient
success upon earth, and the bliss of serving thee in
heaven; through Jesus Christ our Lord.

FOR ALL WHO MOURN 74

Almighty God, Father of all mercies and giver of all comfort: Deal graciously, we pray thee, with those who mourn, that casting every care on thee, they may know the consolation of thy love; through Jesus Christ our Lord.

WHEN THE EVENING COMES 75

O Lord, support us all the day long of this mortal life, until the shades lengthen, and the evening comes, and the busy world is hushed, the fever of life is over, and our work is done. Then, Lord, in thy mercy, grant us safe lodging, a holy rest, and peace at the last; through Jesus Christ our Lord.

A LAST PRAYER 76

Whom have I in heaven but thee: and there is none upon earth that I desire in comparison of thee.

WHY BE HOLY?

77 PRAYER FOR TODAY

Grant us, O Lord, to pass this day in gladness and peace, without stumbling and without stain; that, reaching the eventide victorious over all temptation, we may praise thee, the eternal God, who art blessed, and dost govern all things, world without end.

BIBLE READING *Leviticus* 19:1–2 *and Isaiah* 1:12–17

And the Lord said to Moses, "Say to all the congregation of the people of Israel, You shall be holy; for I the Lord your God am holy."

Meditation: Because God himself is holy, he requires that all who worship him shall be holy too. Church-going and religious observance are not enough: we must cease to do evil, learn to do good, live honestly and try to help all in need.

SILENCE

Prayer: O God, the God of all goodness and 78
grace, who art worthy of a greater love than we
can either give or understand; fill our hearts, we
beseech thee, with such love towards thee as
may cast out all sloth and fear, that nothing may
seem too hard for us to do or suffer in obedience
to thee; and grant that by thus loving, we may
become daily more like unto thee, and finally
obtain the crown of life which thou hast
promised to those who unfeignedly love thee;
through Jesus Christ our Lord.

FOR ALL WHO ADMINISTER JUSTICE 79

O God, mighty and merciful, the judge of all men:
grant to those who minister justice the spirit of
wisdom and discernment; and that they may be
strong and patient, upright and compassionate, fill
them, we beseech thee, with the spirit of thy holy
fear; through Jesus Christ our Lord.

FOR FAMILY LIFE 80

O God our Father, who hast made men to live
together in families: we pray that marriage may be
held in honour, that husbands and wives may live
faithfully together, and that the members of every
family may grow in mutual understanding, in
courtesy and kindness, so that they may bear one
another's burdens, and so fulfil the law of Christ.

TO REMEMBER TODAY 81

O God, grant that the fire of thy holiness may
burn me, until I am holy.

82 PRAISE—FOR GOD'S HOLINESS

> *O worship the Lord in the beauty of holiness:*
> *let the whole earth stand in awe of him.*
> *Tell it out among the nations that the Lord is King:*
> *and that it is he who has made the round world so*
> *fast that it cannot*
> *be moved; and how that he shall judge the people*
> *righteously.*
> *Let the heavens rejoice, and let the earth be glad:*
> *let the sea make a noise, and all that therein is.*
> *Let the field be joyful, and all that is in it:*
> *then shall all the trees of the wood rejoice before the*
> *Lord.*
> *For he cometh, for he cometh to judge the earth:*
> *and with righteousness to judge the world, and the*
> *people with his truth.*

83 PENITENCE

O God, who art a consuming fire of holiness and love, burn me until all evil is consumed—all selfishness, all impurity, all unlove, that I may worship in thy presence and at last be granted the blessing of the pure in heart to see thee in thy holiness, through Jesus Christ my Lord.

84 THE GOSPEL OF HOLINESS

O God, who in holiness and love dost look down upon the sins and perversions of men: Grant that thy church may proclaim the gospel of thy forgiveness and grace, to all in the power of lust and to all who exploit the weaknesses of men and women. Give us love, courage and wisdom in our efforts to help them, and burn up in us all impurity. We ask this for the holiness and love of Jesus Christ, our blessed Lord.

FOR THE SICK   85

O God, the Creator and Father of all men, we praise thee that thy will is life and health and strength. Help all who are ill or in pain to place themselves in thy hands in loving trust, so that thy healing life may flow into them to make them well and strong, able and ready to do thy holy will, through him who has made known to us both thy love and thy will, even Jesus Christ our Lord.

FOR THOSE WHO WATCH   86

Let thy presence, O God, refresh and strengthen all who watch through the night on behalf of others, in sickroom or in hospital: that thy peace may continually possess their souls, and all anxiety may be lifted from their hearts; through Jesus Christ our Lord.

A LAST PRAYER   87

Lord, abide in me, and let me abide in you, so that I may bear much fruit.

THE OTHER MAN

88 BEFORE BIBLE STUDY
Convey to me, O Holy Spirit,
   through the familiar phrases, fresh
      understanding;
   through passages passed over or
      unapprehended, new treasure;
   through thy grace—insight, conviction,
      guidance, revelation, glory.

BIBLE READING   *Leviticus* 19:11–18, 34
You shall not steal, nor deal falsely, nor lie to one
another. . . . You shall do no injustice in judgment
. . . you shall not hate your brother in your heart
. . . the stranger that sojourns with you shall be to
you as the native among you . . . you shall love
your neighbour as yourself.

*Meditation: Here is the second great commandment
picked out by Jesus. Our neighbour is anyone with
whom we are brought into contact, anyone in need of
our help. Our Lord expects us to do to others the same
things that we would like them to do to us. He goes
even further and commands us to love one another, as
he has loved us.*

Prayer: Almighty and most merciful Father, **89** who hast given us a new commandment that we should love one another; give us also grace that we may fulfil it. Make us gentle, courteous, and forbearing. Direct our lives so that we may look each to the good of the other in word and deed. And hallow all our friendships by the blessing of thy Spirit; for his sake who loved us and gave himself for us, Jesus Christ our Lord.

POWER IN TRUST   90

O Lord Jesus Christ, who on thy cross didst overcome the powers of darkness, guide all men who, in seeking knowledge, gain power which can be used for good or evil purposes. Help them to bear their responsibility, and in awe to recognize their stewardship; who livest and reignest, with the Father and the Holy Spirit, God, world without end.

MY WORK TODAY

O Lord, who rewardest every man according to **91** his work, grant me the spirit of honesty and thoroughness; a passion for good craftsmanship; the inspiration of giving, of giving the best, of giving yet more, and not ceasing to give.

TO REMEMBER TODAY   92

If I have not love, I am nothing.

93 THE GOOD NEIGHBOUR

Lord, who shall dwell in thy tabernacle: or who shall rest upon thy holy hill?

Even he, that leadeth an uncorrupt life: and doeth the thing which is right, and speaketh the truth from his heart.

He that hath used no deceit in his tongue, nor done evil to his neighbour: and hath not slandered his neighbour.

He that setteth not by himself, but is lowly in his own eyes: and maketh much of them that fear the Lord.

He that sweareth unto his neighbour, and disappointeth him not: though it were to his own hindrance.

Whoso doeth these things: shall never fall.

94 FOR FORGIVENESS

Almighty and merciful God, the fountain of all goodness, who knowest the thoughts of our hearts, we confess unto thee that we have sinned against thee, and done evil in thy sight. Wash us, we beseech thee, from the stains of our past sins, and give us grace and power to put away all hurtful things; so that, being delivered from the bondage of sin, we may bring forth worthy fruits of repentance, through Jesus Christ our Lord.

95 THE CHURCH AT HOME

O Lord our Saviour, who hast warned us that thou wilt require much from those to whom much is given; grant that we whose lot is cast in so goodly a heritage may strive together the more abundantly to extend to others what we so richly enjoy; and as we have entered into the labours of other men, so to labour that in their turn other men may enter into ours, to the fulfilment of thy holy will and our own everlasting salvation.

FOR COMPASSION 96

O God, we thank thee that some nations in the world are beginning to accept the standards of compassion of our Lord, Jesus Christ. Grant that our nation may give generously for the relief of the homeless and that our people may welcome the refugee into our midst. Help us in our plenty to remember the needs of others and never to grudge the cost of helping them; for his sake who grudged not the death of the cross, but gave himself for all, even Jesus Christ, our Lord.

AN EVENING PRAYER 97

O Lord God, the life of mortals, the light of the faithful, the strength of those who labour, and the repose of the dead; grant us a tranquil night free from all disturbance; that after an interval of quiet sleep, we may, by thy bounty, at the return of light, be endued with activity from the Holy Spirit, and enabled in security to render thanks to thee.

A LAST THOUGHT 98

God is love; and he that abideth in love abideth in God and God in him.

GUILTY, MY LORD

99 A FIRST PRAYER
O Lord, when I awake, and day begins, waken me to thy presence; waken me to thine indwelling; waken me to inward sight of thee, and speech with thee, and strength from thee, that all my earthly walk may waken into song and my spirit leap up to thee all day, all ways.

BIBLE READING   *2 Samuel* 12:1–9
Then David's anger was greatly kindled against the man; and he said to Nathan, "As the Lord lives, the man who has done this deserves to die ..." Nathan said to David, "You are the man."

Meditation: It is much easier to see other people's sins than to recognize our own. Often the sins we condemn most strongly in others are the failures of which we ourselves are guilty. By condemning them in others, we try to deceive ourselves into thinking that we have nothing to do with those particular sins.

SILENCE

Prayer: Forgive me my sins, O Lord, forgive me
the sins of my youth and the sins of mine age,
the sins of my soul, and the sins of my body, my
secret and my whispering sins, my pre-
sumptuous and my crying sins, the sins that I
have done to please myself, and the sins that I
have done to please others. Forgive me those
sins which I know, and those sins which I know
not; forgive them, O Lord, forgive them all, of
thy great goodness.

FOR UNITY OF SPIRIT

O God of peace, who through thy Son Jesus
Christ didst set forth one faith for the salvation of
mankind: Send thy grace and heavenly blessing
upon all Christian people who are striving to draw
nearer to thee and to each other, in the unity of the
spirit and in the bond of peace. Give us penitence
for our divisions, wisdom to know thy truth,
courage to do thy will, love which shall break
down the barriers of prejudice and pride, and an
unswerving loyalty to thy holy name. Unite us all
in thee as thou, O Father, with thy Son and the
Holy Spirit, art one God, world without end.

FOR TODAY

Thou knowest, O God, all that lies before us this
day of duty and of danger and of temptation. Keep
us, we beseech thee, in all things true to thee, that
nothing may come between us and thy holy presence; through Jesus Christ our Lord.

AN ACCEPTABLE PRAYER

God be merciful to me, a sinner.

104 ACT OF PENITENCE

*Have mercy upon me, O God, after thy great goodness:
according to the multitude of thy mercies do away
mine offences. Wash me thoroughly from my wick-
edness: and cleanse me from my sin.*

*For I acknowledge my faults: and my sin is ever before
me. Turn thy face from my sins: and put out all my
misdeeds. Make me a clean heart, O God: and renew
a right spirit within me.*

*Cast me not away from thy presence: and take not thy
holy Spirit from me.*

105 GLORIA

Glory to thee, O God, Creator and Father, for the
universe in which we live, and for men made in
thine own image. Glory to thee, O Christ, who
didst take a human body and didst redeem our
fallen nature. Glory to thee, O Spirit, who dost
make our bodies the temples of thy presence.
Glory to Father, Son and Holy Spirit, whose will
it is that we should be made whole in body, mind
and spirit. Glory to thee to all eternity. Amen.

106 FOR THE CHURCH

Preserve, O God, the catholic church in holiness
and truth, in unity and peace, free from perse-
cution, or glorious under it; that she may advance
the honour of her Lord Jesus, for ever represent his
sacrifice, and glorify his person, and advance his

religion, and be accepted of thee in her blessed Lord, that being filled with his Spirit she may partake of his glory.

Comfort, we beseech thee, most gracious God, all who are cast down and faint of heart amidst the sorrows and difficulties of the world; and grant that, by the energy of thy Holy Spirit, they may be enabled to go upon their way rejoicing and give thee continual thanks for thy sustaining providence; through Jesus Christ our Saviour.

O God, from whom all holy desires, all good counsels, and all just works do proceed: Give unto thy servants that peace which the world cannot give; that both our hearts may be set to obey thy commandments, and also that by thee we being defended from the fear of our enemies may pass our time in rest and quietness; through the merits of Jesus Christ our Saviour.

He who has been forgiven much will love much.

THE VOICE WITHIN

110 INVOCATION

O thou, who art the light of the minds that know thee, the life of the souls that love thee, the strength of the wills that serve thee; help us so to know thee that we may truly love thee; so to love thee that we may fully serve thee, whom to serve is perfect freedom.

BIBLE READING   1 *Kings* 19:9–16

But the Lord was not in the wind ... but the Lord was not in the earthquake ... but the Lord was not in the fire; and after the fire a still small voice. And when Elijah heard it, he wrapped his face in his mantle ... and there came a voice to him.

Meditation: This experience led Elijah to a deeper knowledge of God: God shows himself not so much in the terrifying things of nature—hurricane, earthquake, fire, nor in the upheavals of the world, but in the quiet, gentle voice with which he speaks to the heart of man. That voice moves us to awe and obedience.

SILENCE

Prayer: We pray not, O Lord our God, that thou shouldest reveal thyself by outward signs of mighty works, but in the quiet solitude of our inmost hearts; not by the thunder and the lightning, but by the still small voice; and when thou speakest, give, we beseech thee, to thy servants the hearing ear, and a heart to obey; through Jesus Christ our Lord.

FOR ALL WHO INFLUENCE PUBLIC OPINION

Almighty God, who hast proclaimed thine eternal truth by the voice of prophets and evangelists: Direct and bless, we beseech thee, those who in this our generation speak where many listen and write what many read; that they may do their part in making the heart of the people wise, its mind sound, and its will righteous; to the honour of Jesus Christ our Lord.

LOVE FOR ALL LIVING THINGS

O thou whose divine tenderness ever outsoars the narrow loves and charities of earth, grant me today a kind and gentle heart towards all things that live. Let me not ruthlessly hurt any creature of thine. Let me take thought also for the welfare of little children, and of those who are sick, and of the poor; remembering that what I do unto the least of these his brethren I do unto Jesus Christ my Lord.

TO REMEMBER TODAY

Speak Lord, for thy servant hears.

115   ACT OF WORSHIP

God is our hope and strength: a very present help in trouble. Therefore will we not fear, though the earth be moved: and though the hills be carried into the midst of the sea. Though the waters thereof rage and swell: and though the mountains shake at the tempest of the same. The nations make much ado, and the kingdoms are moved: but God hath shewed his voice, and the earth shall melt away. Be still then, and know that I am God: I will be exalted among the nations, and I will be exalted in the earth.

116   MUCH FORGIVEN

Give us, O Lord, a humble spirit, that we may never presume upon thy mercy, but live always as those who have been much forgiven. Make us tender and compassionate toward those who are overtaken by temptation, considering ourselves, how we have fallen in times past and may fall yet again. Make us watchful and sober-minded, looking ever unto thee for grace to stand upright, and to persevere unto the end; through thy Son Jesus Christ our Lord.

117   FOR THE MINISTERS OF THE CHURCH

O Lord Jesus Christ, who dost call men to serve thee as ministers in thy church; make them to be men of God, men of prayer, holy and humble of heart, faithful shepherds of thy flock. Grant that they may lead us to thee in true worship and loving service; help us to support them by our prayers and efforts, so that thy good will may be done. We ask this of thee, O Lord and Master, who dost live and reign with the Father and the Holy Spirit, one God blessed for evermore.

FOR THE SLEEPLESS 118

Gracious and most merciful Father; let thy presence and peace be known wheresoever there is sickness, sorrow or distress. Give to all tired and weary sufferers, this night, the gift of sleep; and, if sleep come not, let thy Holy Spirit bring to their remembrance thoughts of comfort from thy word, that they may stay their minds on thee, through Jesus Christ our Lord.

A PRAYER FOR CLEANSING 119

Lord, ere I sleep I pray thy Spirit to cleanse and sanctify the impulses and memories of this day, that nought may go down into the depth of my being which has not been marked as thine. So give me true and holy being in the new creation of Jesus Christ, thy well-beloved Son.

A LAST PRAYER 120

Thy gentleness hath made me great.

WHEN WE WORSHIP

121 PREPARATION
Be thou master of my heart and mind when I pray,
O my Lord. Keep my thoughts ever fixed on thee,
so that my prayer may be directed to thy glory.
May the thoughts that enrapture thy saints in
heaven fill me with joy, and let me love and adore
thee always.

BIBLE READING   *Isaiah* 6:1–8
Holy, holy, holy is the Lord of hosts; the whole
earth is full of his glory ... and I said: "Woe is me!
For I am lost; for I am a man of unclean lips ... for
my eyes have seen the King, the Lord of hosts!"

*Meditation: The vision of God's burning holiness
makes us see ourselves as we really are, as God sees
us. Our first thought is one of despair, so great is the
gap between God and ourselves. Then God cleanses
and forgives, strengthens and sanctifies us, and gives
us work to do for him.*

SILENCE

Prayer: Lord God Almighty, who hast given to 122
us the vision of thy holiness, and therewith of
our unworthiness to be thy witnesses: Touch,
we pray thee, our lips with thy cleansing fire;
that so cleansed and hallowed, we may go forth
amongst men as those whom thou hast sent; for
Jesus Christ's sake.

FOR OUR NATION 123

O God, the God of all righteousness, mercy, and
love; Give us grace and strength to conceive and
execute whatever be for thine honour and the
welfare of the nation; that we may become at last,
through the merits and intercession of our common Redeemer, a great and a happy, because a
wise and understanding people; to thy honour and
glory.

THE WORSHIP OF HEAVEN 124

O God, who hast brought us near to an innumerable company of angels and to the spirits of just
men made perfect; grant us during our earthly
pilgrimage to abide in their fellowship, and in our
heavenly country to become partakers of their
joy; through Jesus Christ our Lord.

TO REMEMBER TODAY 125

Take heart, my son; your sins are forgiven.

126 WORSHIP IN HEAVEN AND EARTH

We praise thee, O God: we acknowledge thee to be the Lord.

All the earth doth worship thee: the Father everlasting.

To thee all Angels cry aloud: the heavens and all the powers therein.

To thee Cherubin, and Seraphin: continually do cry,

Holy, Holy, Holy: Lord God of Sabaoth;

Heaven and earth are full of the Majesty of thy glory.

127 FALLING SHORT

O most holy God, as I look back upon this day I see how often I have failed thee, how sadly I fall short of thy glory for me. As I remember what I have been, what I am even now, my heart fails me. Speak to my heart the healing words, "Thy sins are forgiven thee"; cleanse and sanctify me; give me thy grace that I may resist every temptation to evil and obey only thy holy will, through him who came into the world to save sinners, even Jesus Christ my Lord and Saviour.

128 FOR THE LAITY

Almighty and everlasting God, by whose Spirit the whole body of the church is governed and sanctified: Receive our supplications and prayers, which we offer before thee for all estates of men in thy holy church, that every member of the same, in his vocation and ministry, may truly and in godly manner serve thee; through our Lord and Saviour Jesus Christ.

We ask thee not, O Lord, to rid us of pain; but grant in thy mercy that our pain may be free from waste, unfretted by rebellion against thy will, unsoiled by thoughts of ourselves, purified by love of our kind, and ennobled by devotion to thy kingdom; through the merits of thine only Son our Lord.

Almighty God, help us as the day departs, to enter thy secret place where there is no darkness at all. Disperse the shadows that hide thy glory from us, and illumine our souls with the radiance of thy truth and love; through Jesus Christ our Lord.

Grant, O Lord, that at the last, I may be found worthy to worship with thy saints and angels, and to see the glory of thy face.

A NEW CONTRACT

132 FOR TRUE WORSHIP
O Almighty God, from whom every good prayer cometh, and who pourest out on all who desire it the spirit of grace and supplication: Deliver us, when we draw nigh to thee, from coldness of heart and wanderings of mind, that with steadfast thoughts and kindled affections we may worship thee in spirit and in truth; through Jesus Christ our Lord.

BIBLE READING   *Jeremiah* 31:31–34
"Behold, the days are coming, says the Lord, when I will make a new covenant with the house of Israel ... I will put my law within them, and I will write it upon their hearts; and I will be their God, and they shall be my people ... for they shall all know me, from the least of them to the greatest."

Meditation: The new covenant longed for by Jeremiah was fulfilled by Jesus and sealed by his death. The Spirit of God now lives within us, enabling us to know God and to live according to his will.

Prayer: O Almighty God, whom truly to know 133
is everlasting life: Grant us perfectly to know
thy Son Jesus Christ to be the way, the truth,
and the life; that following the steps of thy holy
apostles, we may steadfastly walk in the way
that leadeth to eternal life; through the same thy
Son Jesus Christ our Lord.

FOR ETERNAL VALUES   134
Deliver us, O God, from following the fashions of
the day in our thinking. Save us from the worship
of power, whether power over nature or power
over man; save us from the worship of science,
and grant that, giving thee thanks for the skill of
the scientist, we may be preserved from the abuse
of his discoveries. Help us never to confuse any
creature with the Creator, or man with God. May
we acknowledge man's reason as thy gift and,
being freed from all false hopes and misplaced
trust, find in thee our hope and our salvation,
through Jesus Christ our Lord.

TO REMEMBER TODAY   135
This is eternal life, to know thee the only true
God, and Jesus Christ whom thou hast sent.

136 THE WONDER OF GOD'S LAW

The Law of the Lord is an undefiled law, converting the soul: the testimony of the Lord is sure, and giveth wisdom unto the simple.

The statutes of the Lord are right, and rejoice the heart: the commandment of the Lord is pure, and giveth light unto the eyes.

The fear of the Lord is clean, and endureth for ever: the judgments of the Lord are true, and righteous altogether.

More to be desired are they than gold, yea, than much fine gold: sweeter also than honey, and the honeycomb.

Moreover, by them is thy servant taught: and in keeping of them there is great reward.

Who can tell how oft he offendeth? O cleanse thou me from my secret faults.

Let the words of my mouth, and the meditation of my heart: be always acceptable in thy sight,

O Lord: my strength, and my redeemer.

137 PARDON AND PEACE

Grant, we beseech thee, merciful Lord, to thy faithful people pardon and peace, that they may be cleansed from all their sins, and serve thee with a quiet mind; through Jesus Christ our Lord.

Most gracious Father, we humbly beseech thee for thy holy catholic church: Fill it with all truth; in all truth with all peace. Where it is corrupt, purge it; where it is in error, direct it; where anything is amiss, reform it; where it is right, strengthen and confirm it; where it is in want, furnish it; where it is divided and rent asunder, make up the breaches of it, O thou Holy One of Israel.

FOR "INCURABLES"   **139**

O heavenly Father, we pray thee for those suffering from diseases for which at present there is no cure. Give them the victory of trust and hope, that they may never lose their faith in thy loving purpose. Grant thy wisdom to all who are working to discover the causes of disease, and the realization that through thee all things are possible. We ask this in the name of him who went about doing good and healing all manner of disease, even thy Son Jesus Christ our Lord.

A LAST PRAYER   **140**

God be in my head and in my understanding; God be in my eyes and in my looking; God be in my mouth and in my speaking; God be in my heart and in my thinking; God be at my end and at my departing.

CITY OF PEACE

141 GOD OUR HOPE AND JOY

My God and my Lord, thou art my hope and my heart's joy. Thou hast made me in thine image, that I may direct all my thoughts to thee, and love thee aright, that I may more and more love thee, enjoy thee, and possess thee. Let my love to thee grow in this life, and let it ripen in the life to come, my God and my Lord.

BIBLE READING   *Micah* 4:1–4

It shall come to pass in the latter days that the mountain of the house of the Lord shall be established as the highest of the mountains ... and peoples shall flow to it ... and they shall beat their swords into ploughshares, and their spears into pruning hooks; nation shall not lift up sword against nation, neither shall they learn war any more.

Meditation: A vision which will only be fulfilled when men learn the ways of God. Jesus wept over Jerusalem, because it did not know the things that make for peace—truth, justice, freedom and brotherhood. When people put God's will before narrow nationalisms, there will be peace.

Prayer: Lord, make us instruments of thy peace. **142**
Where there is hatred, let us sow love;
where there is injury, pardon;
where there is discord, union;
where there is doubt, faith;
where there is despair, hope;
where there is darkness, light;
where there is sadness, joy;
for thy mercy and for thy truth's sake.

RIGHT USE OF POWER

Almighty and merciful God, without whom all **143**
things hasten to destruction and fall into nothing-
ness: Look, we beseech thee, upon thy family of
nations and men, to which thou hast committed
power in truth for their mutual health and comfort. Save us and help us, O Lord, lest we abuse
thy gift and make it our misery and ruin; draw all
men unto thee in thy kingdom of righteousness
and truth; uproot our enmities, heal our divisions,
cast out our fears; and renew our faith in thine
unchanging purpose of goodwill and peace on
earth; for the love of Jesus Christ our Lord.

TO REMEMBER TODAY **144**

Thou wilt keep him in perfect peace whose mind
is stayed on thee.

145　CITY OF PEACE

I was glad when they said unto me:
We will go into the house of the Lord.
Our feet shall stand at thy gates:
O Jerusalem.
O pray for the peace of Jerusalem:
they shall prosper that love thee.
Peace be within thy walls:
and plenteousness within thy palaces.
For my brethren and companions' sakes:
I will wish thee prosperity.
Yea, because of the house of the Lord our God:
I will seek to do thee good.

146　PENITENCE FOR SOCIAL INJUSTICE

Almighty God, who hast entrusted this earth unto the children of men, and through thy Son Jesus Christ hast called us unto a heavenly citizenship: Grant us, we humbly beseech thee, such shame and repentance for the disorder and injustice and cruelty which are among us, that, fleeing unto thee for pardon and for grace, we may henceforth set ourselves to establish that city which has justice for its foundation and love for its law, whereof thou art the architect and maker; through the same Lord Jesus Christ, thy Son, our Saviour.

O God, we pray thee for thy church which is set today amid the perplexities of a changing order, and is face to face with a new task; Fill us all afresh with the Spirit of Pentecost; help us to proclaim boldly the coming of thy kingdom; and do thou hasten the time when the knowledge of thyself shall fill the earth, as the waters cover the sea.

FOR THOSE IN TRIAL 148

Have mercy, O Lord, upon those who are passing through sore trial: the poor, the sick, the anxious, the oppressed; those who are in danger from the fury of the elements, or from the violence of men. Inspire in us, and in our fellow men, the will to help our suffering brethren. Heal, protect, and strengthen them, according to their need. Comfort those in sorrow, with the comfort which is in Christ Jesus our Lord.

FOR THE WORLD'S SAKE 149

O Lord Christ, for the world's sake
Thou didst stand against the world;
Grant that I too may stand for the world
against the world; and love the world
with something of thy great love.

A LAST PRAYER 150

Now may the blessing of God rest and remain upon his people, in every land, of every tongue.

THE SPIRIT FOR ALL

151 BEFORE BIBLE STUDY

O Lord God, who hast lent unto us thy holy word to be a lantern unto our feet, and a light unto our steps: give unto us all thy Holy Spirit, that out of the same word we may learn what is thy eternal will, and frame our lives in all holy obedience to the same, to thy honour and glory and increase of our faith; through Jesus Christ our Lord.

BIBLE READING   *Joel* 2:28, 29

And it shall come to pass afterward, that I will pour out my spirit on all flesh; your sons and your daughters shall prophesy, your old men shall dream dreams, and your young men shall see visions. Even upon the menservants and maidservants in those days, I will pour out my spirit.

Meditation: Through Jesus Christ the Holy Spirit is available for all, not just for the selected few. Ordinary men and women can be filled with God's Spirit and be raised to new possibilities, as were the apostles on the day of Pentecost and afterwards.

SILENCE

Prayer: O Holy Spirit, giver of light and life, 152
impart to us thoughts higher than our own
thoughts, and prayers better than our own
prayers, and powers beyond our own powers,
that we may spend and be spent in the ways of
love and goodness, after the perfect image of
our Lord and Saviour Jesus Christ.

THE SPIRIT'S DIRECTION   153
O God, who art the goal of all knowledge and the
source of all truth, who dost lead mankind
towards thyself along the paths of discovery and
learning, direct with thy wise Spirit the work of
education in every land. Especially we would pray
for those who have the difficult task of adapting
new knowledge to the mind of ancient peoples.
Give them insight into the needs of those whom
they teach, humility to learn from their traditions,
and wisdom to combine the old and the new.
Above all, give them that grace and beauty of life
without which all knowledge is vain.

TO REMEMBER TODAY   154
God's love has been poured into our hearts
through the Holy Spirit which has been given to
us.

155 ST. PAUL'S PRAYER

For this reason I bow my knees before the Father, from
whom every family in heaven and on earth is named,
that according to the riches of his glory he may grant you
to be strengthened with might through his Spirit in the
inner man, and that Christ may dwell in your hearts
through faith; that you, being rooted and grounded in
love, may have power to comprehend with all the saints
what is the breadth and length and height and depth, and
to know the love of Christ which surpasses knowledge,
that you may be filled with all the fullness of God.

156 IN THE DEPTHS OF BEING

O Spirit of God,
who dost speak to spirits
created in thine own likeness,
Penetrate into the depth of our spirits
into the storehouse of memories
remembered and forgotten,
into the depths of being,
the very springs of personality
And cleanse and forgive
Making us whole and holy
That we may be thine
And live in the new being
of Christ our Lord.

O Holy Spirit of God, who on the day of Pentecost didst unify the language of men so that thy messengers were able to speak to the heart of men of many nations and draw them to thee: Grant to thy church in our generation so to enter into the experience and thinking of men that its message may go home to their hearts, and make known the saving love of him who from his cross is ever drawing all men to himself, even Jesus Christ, the Lord of all and the Saviour of all.

FOR A SICK FRIEND 158

Lord, he whom thou lovest is sick: we need say no more and worry no more. Do for him according to his need—hold him with thy hand in thine unfailing love—him whom we love and whom thou lovest.

PEACE OF SOUL 159

Lord Jesus, by thine own peace of soul, rooted and living in the eternal Father, serene in the hours of commotion and anguish, grant me thy tranquillity. Be my life hid in thine; let thy fearless and imperturbable Spirit come to dwell in mine and be my peace.

A LAST THOUGHT 160

Peace I leave with you, my peace I give unto you.

THE GREAT MOMENT

161 A MORNING PRAYER

O gracious Father, since it is of thy mercy that another day is added to our lives; we here dedicate both our souls and bodies to thee and thy service, in a sober. righteous and godly life: in which resolution, do thou, O merciful God, confirm and strengthen us; that, as we grow in age, we may grow in grace, and in the knowledge of our Lord and Saviour, Jesus Christ.

BIBLE READING   *Luke 2:1–7*

And while they were there, the time came for her to be delivered. And she gave birth to her first-born son and wrapped him in swaddling cloths, and laid him in a manger, because there was no place for them in the inn.

Meditation: God comes to men with all the humility of Bethlehem. He puts himself into the hands of men as a helpless babe to show them that they need not fear him. He was born in an inn, where all men could come; in a stable where even the animals had a place. Saviour of all.

SILENCE

Prayer: Lord, let me kneel before thy miracle 162
　　　　　　—an infant in a stable
　　　　　　　on a human mother's breast,
　　　　　　from all eternity thine only begotten
　　　　　　　　Son,
　　　　　　　thy Word from before beginning,
　　　　　　God of God, Light of Light,
　　　　　　　　Very God of Very God,
　　　　　　　of his own choice, of thine own
　　　　　　　　purpose,
　　　　　　　　　made mortal man.

FOR CHILDREN AND PARENTS 163

Heavenly Father, after whom all fatherhood in heaven and earth is named: bless, we beseech thee, all children, and give to their parents and to all in whose charge they may be, the spirit of wisdom and love: so that the home in which they grow up may be to them an image of thy kingdom, and the care of their parents a likeness of thy love; through Jesus Christ our Lord.

OFFERINGS FOR BETHLEHEM 164

O God our Father, who through the gift of thy Holy Spirit hast hung forth a star in the lowly heaven of every Christian soul, grant us with eager feet to follow whither it leads, bringing for gold, frankincense and myrrh the offering of ourselves, our souls and bodies, for the love of thy Son, Jesus Christ our Lord.

TO REMEMBER TODAY 165

No one has ever seen God; the only Son, who is in the bosom of the Father, he has made him known.

166 PRAISE FOR BETHLEHEM

Glory be to God on high,
and in earth peace, good will towards men.
We praise thee, we bless thee,
We worship thee, we glorify thee,
We give thanks to thee for thy great glory,
O Lord God, heavenly king,
God the Father Almighty.

167 A NEW BIRTH

O Christ, whose wondrous birth meaneth nothing unless we be born again, whose death and sacrifice nothing unless we die unto sin, whose resurrection nothing if thou be risen alone: Raise and exalt us, O Saviour, both now to the estate of grace and hereafter to the state of glory; where with the Father and the Holy Spirit thou livest and reignest, God for ever and ever.

168 GOOD NEWS

O Lord Jesus Christ, who hast commanded us to make known the good news of thy love to all nations: Help us so to experience thy forgiveness, grace and peace that we may want all other people to share those blessings also and to come into the family of thy Father, to whom be all gratitude, love and praise for ever and ever.

FOR SUFFERING CHILDREN

O God, our Father, we remember before thee all orphaned, homeless, and unwanted children, the children of loveless homes, and those who suffer from bodily defect and disease. Make our hearts burn within us for the children of our dark places, and teach us how to turn to good account the laws that protect them and the efforts of those who strive to succour them; through Jesus Christ our Lord.

FOR ABSENT FRIENDS

O God, who art present to thy faithful people in every place, mercifully hear our prayers for those we love who are now parted from us: watch over them, we beseech thee, and protect them in anxiety, danger, and temptation; and assure both them and us that thou art always near, and that we are one in thee for ever; through Jesus Christ our Lord.

CLOSING WORSHIP

To thy name, Lord Jesus, help me to bow the knee
and all its worshipping,
bow the head
and all its thinking,
bow the will
and all its choosing,
bow the heart
and all its loving.

THE DIVINE PROGRAMME

172 FOR GOD'S PROTECTION

O Almighty and most merciful God, of thy bountiful goodness keep us, we beseech thee, from all things that may hurt us; that we, being ready both in body and soul, may cheerfully accomplish those things which thou commandest; through Jesus Christ our Lord.

BIBLE READING   *Luke* 4:16–21 (*Isaiah* 61:1–2)

The Spirit of the Lord is upon me, because the Lord has anointed me to bring good tidings to the afflicted; to bind up the brokenhearted, to proclaim liberty to the captives, and the opening of the prison to those who are bound; to proclaim the year of the Lord's favour.

Meditation: This is the text which our Lord chose to be the purpose of his mission. It was perfectly fulfilled in him, both the ministry of love and the anointing of the Spirit. He brings freedom to men in all their prisons—of despair, pain, sin and difficulty, and gives us the glorious liberty of the children of God.

SILENCE

173 *Prayer:* Grant, O Lord, that this mind may be in us, which was also in Christ Jesus, who left the heaven of thy holiness and of thy glory that he might take upon him our sins and our sorrows, and seek and save that which was lost. Stir the hearts of thy people that they may multiply their labours in the cause of charity and love, that they may minister to the wants of others, and by their good works lead many to glorify our Father in heaven; through Jesus Christ our Lord.

FOR ALL IN COMMERCE AND INDUSTRY 174

O God, who givest to every man his work and through his labours dost accomplish thy purposes upon earth: Grant thy blessing, we beseech thee, to those who are engaged in the industries and commerce of this land. Inspire them with the knowledge that in ministering to the needs of others they are serving thee; defend them from injustice and greed, and give them the due reward of their labours; that, seeking first thy kingdom and thy righteousness, all things may be added unto them here and hereafter; through Jesus Christ our Lord.

FOR COURTESY 175

O God, who through the life of thy Son hast shown the dignity of service: Help us to be courteous and considerate to all those who serve us in shops and offices, on our journeys, and in our homes; that all labour may be held in honour and our people may be united in mutual respect, to the glory of thy name.

TO REMEMBER TODAY 176

Lo, I come to do thy will, O my God: I delight to do it; yea, thy law is within my heart.

177 ACT OF PRAISE

Blessed be the Lord God of Israel:
for he hath visited, and redeemed his people;
And hath raised up a mighty salvation for us:
in the house of his servant David;
To give knowledge of salvation unto his people:
for the remission of their sins,
Through the tender mercy of our God:
whereby the day-spring from on high hath visited us.

178 CONFESSION

Merciful God, we humble ourselves in thy presence, confessing our unworthiness and sinfulness in thy sight. We have broken thy holy law. We have not sought first thy kingdom and thy righteousness. We have been anxious and troubled about many things, and have neglected the things that belong to our peace. We have not loved our neighbour as ourselves, or done to others as we would that they should do to us. Forgive us, we beseech thee, and renew a right spirit within us, through the grace of Jesus Christ our Lord.

179 FOR THE WHOLE CHURCH

Remember, O Lord, thy holy catholic and apostolic church, which is from one end of the earth to the other; all peoples and all thy flocks. Vouchsafe to all our hearts the peace which is from heaven, and also bestow upon us the peace of this life. For thou art our God, he that sets free the bound, he that raises those that are in misery, the hope of the hopeless, the succour of the defenceless, the resurrection of the fallen, and the harbour of the tempest-tossed. Thine is the kingdom and the power and the glory.

FOR THE SICK IN MIND 180

O Holy Spirit who dost search out all things, even the deep things of God and the deep things of man, we pray thee so to penetrate into the springs of personality of all who are sick in mind, to bring them cleansing, healing and unity. Sanctify all memory, dispel all fear, and bring them to love thee with all their mind and will, that they may be made whole and glorify thee for ever. We ask this in the name of him who cast out devils and healed men's minds, even Jesus Christ our Lord.

AGLOW WITH CHRIST'S SPIRIT 181

Grant me, O God, tranquillity of mind and soul out of a faith settled and lively, secure from the world's fevers, serene in the knowledge of thy nearness, and of thy perfect, unchanging will; dwelling in the light eternal and the truth invisible, aglow with Christ's Spirit, and Christ's love.

A LAST PRAYER 182

May the peace of God which passes all understanding guard our hearts and minds in Christ Jesus.

EASY—WITH HIM

183 READY TO LEARN

Thou alone, O God, art inexhaustible, and ever offerest me something new to know, something new to love. . . . And so on for eternity I shall ever be a little child beginning to be taught the lessons of thy infinite divine nature.

BIBLE READING   *Matthew* 11:28–30

Come to me, all who labour and are heavy-laden, and I will give you rest. Take my yoke upon you, and learn from me; for I am gentle and lowly in heart, and you will find rest for your souls. For my yoke is easy, and my burden is light.

> *Meditation: A yoke helps the ox to pull the plough or the cart without chafing or strain. Our Lord gives us his yoke to help us bear our burdens—gentleness and lowliness of heart. If we are trusting enough to go to him, he will give us rest and strength.*

SILENCE

Prayer: Let us not seek out of thee what we can
only find in thee, O Lord!
Peace and rest and joy and bliss,
which abide only in thine abiding
joy.
Lift up our souls above the weary
round of
harassing thoughts to thy eternal
presence.
Lift up our mind to the pure, bright,
serene
atmosphere of thy presence,
that we may breathe freely,
there repose in thy love,
there be at rest from ourselves
and from all things that weary
us:
and thence return, arrayed in thy
peace,
to do and bear
whatsoever shall best please
thee.

CHRIST'S YOKE-FELLOW   185

Where deed of mine this day can help to make this
world a better place for men to live in, where
word of mine can cheer a despondent heart or
brace a weak will, where prayer of mine can hasten the coming of Christ's kingdom, there let me
do and speak and pray.

TO REMEMBER TODAY   186

I can do all things through him who strengthens
me.

187 A PSALM OF TRUST

Hear me when I call, O God of my righteousness: thou hast set me at liberty when I was in trouble; have mercy upon me, and hearken unto my prayer.

Offer the sacrifice of righteousness: and put your trust in the Lord.

There be many that say: Who will shew us any good?

Lord lift thou up: the light of thy countenance upon us.

Thou hast put gladness in my heart: since the time that their corn, and wine, and oil, increased.

I will lay me down in peace, and take my rest: for it is thou, Lord, only, that makest me dwell in safety.

188 COVER OUR SINS

Into thy hands, O gracious Father, we commend ourselves, and all whom we love. Thine, O Lord, is the day, thine also is the night; cover our sins with thy mercy as thou dost cover the earth with darkness; and grant that the sun of righteousness may ever shine in our hearts, to chase away the darkness of all evil thoughts; through Jesus Christ our Lord.

O thou, who art the light of the world, the desire of all nations, and the shepherd of our souls: let thy light shine in the darkness, that all the ends of the earth may see the salvation of our God. By the lifting up of thy cross gather the peoples to thine obedience; let thy sheep hear thy voice, and be brought home to thy fold; so that there may be one flock, one shepherd, one holy kingdom of righteousness and peace, one God and Father of all, above all, and in all, and through all.

BURDEN BEARING   190

Give me a stout heart to bear my own burdens. Give me a willing heart to bear the burdens of others. Give me a believing heart to cast all burdens upon thee, O Lord my God.

GRATITUDE FOR LOVE   191

Blessed be thou for all whom I have loved, and who have loved me: And for thy love, from all eternity, beyond compare or compass: merciful, tender, unalterable, irremovable. Blessed be thou, O Lord.

A LAST THOUGHT   192

Casting all your care upon him, for he careth for you.

ALL WE NEED TO KNOW

193   A MORNING PRAYER

O Lord our heavenly Father, Almighty and ever-lasting God, who hast safely brought us to the beginning of this day: Defend us today with thy mighty power; and grant that this day we fall into no sin, neither run into any kind of danger; but that all our doings may be ordered by thy governance, to do always that is righteous in thy sight; through Jesus Christ our Lord.

BIBLE READING   *John* 14:1–6

Jesus said to him, "I am the way, and the truth, and the life; no one comes to the Father, but by me."

Meditation: Christ shows us all that we need to know about God, man and the world; if we follow and obey him we shall come to God; all spiritual life comes from him, sufficient for our every need. If we know him intimately from our study of the gospels and from our daily touch with him, we gain eternal life—our Lord's own life.

SILENCE

Prayer: O Lord Jesus Christ, 194
>   who art the way, the truth, and the
>   life;
>   we pray thee
>   suffer us not to stray from thee, who art
>   the way,
>   nor to distrust thee who art the truth,
>   nor to rest in any other thing than thee,
>   who art the life.
>   Teach us by thy Holy Spirit
>   what to believe,
>   what to do,
>   and wherein to take our rest.
>   For thine own name's sake we ask it.

FOR ABSENT FRIENDS 195

O God, the Father and defender of thy people, whom neither space nor time can separate from such as continue in thy keeping; be present, we beseech thee, with those who are parted from us; prosper them and do them good; guide and direct them in all their undertakings; let nothing hurtful beset them and no evil befall them; and grant that, upheld by thy right hand, they may arrive in safety at their journey's end; through Jesus Christ our Lord.

TO REMEMBER TODAY 196

Lord, to whom shall we go? You have the words of eternal life.

197   ACT OF PRAISE

Thy mercy, O Lord, reacheth unto the heavens: and thy faithfulness unto the clouds.

Thy righteousness standeth like the strong mountains: thy judgments are like the great deep.

Thou, Lord, shalt save both man and beast; How excellent is thy mercy, O God: and the children of men shall put their trust under the shadow of thy wings.

They shall be satisfied with the plenteousness of thy house: and thou shalt give them drink of thy pleasures, as out of the river.

For with thee is the well of life: and in thy light shall we see light.

O continue forth thy lovingkindness unto them that know thee: and thy righteousness unto them that are true of heart.

198   SINS AGAINST TRUTH

O God, who desirest truth in the inmost heart, forgive me my sins against truth—the untruth within me, the half-lies, the evasions, the exaggerations, the lying silences, the self-deceits, the masks I wear before the world. Let me stand naked before thee, and see myself as I really am. Then, grant me truth in the inward parts and keep me in truth always.

FOR THE CHURCH

O God, rouse thy church, lest we sleep and miss men's need of thee and thy yearning love for men. O God, cleanse thy church and forgive our lack of zeal for thy kingdom. O God, set thy church ablaze with the fire of thy Spirit, that we may spend and be spent for thy gospel, thy will and thy glory, through all our days.

FOR THE TEMPTED

O God of all power and love, who didst send thine angel to strengthen my Lord in his temptation and agony: strengthen all who are in temptation tonight, all in agony, and all the dying, and give them victory and peace, through him who overcame, even Jesus Christ our Lord.

THE PILGRIM WAY

Control me, O my God, gently, pervasively, irresistibly, increasingly, so that I walk my pilgrim way steadily and in a sure light; so that I neither dally nor disobey, nor slip down, nor stand still, nor sink down. Control me, O my God.

A LAST THOUGHT

They that wait upon the Lord shall renew their strength.

FOOD FOR LIFE

203 FOR TODAY

O Lord of light, make pure our hearts, that we may see thee; reveal thyself to us, that we may love thee. Strengthen our wills, that we may choose the good from the evil, and day by day manifest in the world the glory and power of thy blessed gospel, which thou hast made known to us through thy Son Jesus Christ.

BIBLE READING   *John* 6:31–35

I am the bread of life; he who comes to me shall not hunger, and he who believes in me shall never thirst.

> *Meditation: Our spirits need food as much as our bodies. Our Lord shares with us his own life which has conquered all difficulties, temptations, hardships, and death itself. Every time we touch him in prayer, every time we meet him in Holy Communion, his life passes into us to cleanse, strengthen and invigorate us.*

SILENCE

Prayer: O Lord,

> Make me to hunger after thy
> heavenly food,
> which is thyself,
> denied to none that comes.
> That life given for the life of the
> world,
> mingle now with mine;
> not according to my feeble
> desire
> but according to thy love.

FOR FARMERS

Give, O Lord, to all who till the ground
wisdom to understand thy laws,
and to co-operate with thy wise ordering
of the world:
and grant that the bountiful fruits of the earth
may not be hoarded by the selfish
or squandered by the foolish,
but that all who work may share abundantly
in the harvest of the soil;
through Jesus Christ our Lord.

TO REMEMBER TODAY

Man does not live by bread alone, but man lives by
everything that proceeds out of the mouth of God.

207 EVENING PRAISE

*The eyes of all wait upon thee, O Lord: and thou givest
them their meat in due season.*

*Thou openest thine hand: and fillest all things living
with plenteousness.*

*The Lord is righteous in all his ways: and holy in all
his works.*

*The Lord is nigh unto all them that call upon him: yea,
all such as call upon him faithfully.*

*He will fulfil the desire of them that fear him: he also
will hear their cry, and will help them.*

*My mouth shall speak the praise of the Lord: and let all
flesh give thanks unto his holy Name for ever and
ever.*

208 THE DOOR OF THY MERCY

O God, I knock at the door of thy mercy with the
hand of my hope, I flee unto thee, seeking refuge
from my multiplied sins, and I hang upon the
borders of thy garment with the fingers of my
trust. So pardon, O God, the wrongs I have done,
the evils and the sins, and rid me, O God, of my
evil state, for thou art my Lord and sovereign, my
reliance and my hope.

209 THE SINS OF THE CHURCHES

O Lord Jesus Christ, thy body was broken on the
cross by the sins of the world; thy body is broken
now by the sins of the church. Forgive the world

the sins it knew not, and make the church know the sin it is doing to thee. Bring us all to penitence and unity in thee for the world's sake.

FOR THE HUNGRY

O heavenly Father, who by thy blessed Son hast taught us to ask of thee our daily bread; have compassion on the millions of our fellow men who live in poverty and hunger; relieve their distress; make plain the way of help; and grant thy grace unto us all, that we may bear each other's burdens according to thy will; through Jesus Christ our Lord.

THE GOODNESS OF GOD

O my God, thou art good:
there is none good but thee;
all greatness thou art, but all goodness first.
Out of thy goodness thou madest me;
for thy goodness I know thee;
after thy goodness would I walk;
to the kingdom of thy goodness, come.
My mouth shall speak of thy goodness all the
day long,
for I know no end thereof.

A LAST PRAYER

Into thy faithful hands, O God, we commit ourselves and all whom we love now and always.

LIGHT ON HIS FEET

213   A MORNING PRAYER

Give us trust in thee, O God, for all that today shall bring. Enable us cheerfully to perform our appointed duties, and, without murmuring or reluctance, to do whatsoever thy will directs. Be our strength in weakness, our light in darkness, our wisdom in uncertainty; and grant us full assurance that neither death nor life, nor things present nor things to come, shall be able to separate us from thy love in Christ Jesus our Lord.

BIBLE READING   *John* 8:12; 1 *John* 1:5–7
I am the light of the world; he who follows me will not walk in darkness but will have the light of life.

> *Meditation: Christ always goes before us in the dark and difficult journeys of life. His light shows up his own feet so that we may tread in his footsteps. He is not only the light on a dark night, but the sun of the full day.*

SILENCE

Prayer: O thou to whom we always look,
   lighten our hearts
   as the sun throws light
  upon the dark bushes around us.
 May we always reflect thy radiance
  so that those who have not known
    thee
   may see thee in us.
 In the name of the great light we ask
   this.

FOR TRAVELLERS BY ROAD

Almighty God, giver of life and health, guide, we pray thee, with thy wisdom all who are striving to save from injury and death the travellers on our roads. Grant to those who drive along the highways consideration for others, and to those who walk on them or play beside them thoughtful caution and care; that so without fear or disaster we all may come safely to our journey's end, by thy mercy who carest for us; through Jesus Christ our Lord.

ON GOING FORTH

Oh send out thy light and thy truth; let them lead me, let them bring me to thy holy hill and to thy dwelling!

217 ACT OF TRUST

The Lord is my light and my salvation; whom then
  shall I fear? the Lord is the strength of my life; of
  whom then shall I be afraid?

Though an host of men were laid against me, yet shall
  not my heart be afraid: and though there rose up war
  against me, yet will I put my trust in him.

One thing have I desired of the Lord, which I will
  require: even that I may dwell in the house of the
  Lord all the days of my life, to behold the fair beauty
  of the Lord, and to visit his temple.

For in the time of trouble he shall hide me in his
  tabernacle: yea, in the secret place of his dwelling
  shall he hide me, and set me up upon a rock of stone.

Therefore will I offer in his dwelling an oblation with
  great gladness: I will sing, and speak praises unto the
  Lord.

218 SECRET SINS

O most holy God, forgive my secret ambitions,
my secret self-seeking, my secret lusts, which I
hide from men, but cannot hide from thee. Forgive, and cleanse, and make me new, through
Jesus Christ.

219 OUR LOCAL CHURCH

O Lord Jesus Christ, who didst go, as thy custom
was, into the synagogue on the sabbath day,
quicken with thy abiding presence the life of thy
church in our country; that every church may be
as a city set upon a hill, a witness to thy claims

upon our worship and service, a power-house of prayer, a community of love, and a joy and comfort to thy servants. Hear us from thy throne in heaven, where with the Father and the Holy Spirit thou livest and reignest, one God, world without end.

FOR THE BLIND 220

O God, who art the Father of lights, with whom is no darkness at all: we thank thee for the good gift of sight which thou hast bestowed upon us. Fill us, we pray thee, with thine own compassion for those who have it not; direct and prosper the efforts that are made for their welfare: reveal to them by thy Spirit the things which eye hath not seen and comfort them with the hope of the light everlasting; to which, of thy great mercy, we beseech thee to bring us all; through Jesus Christ our Saviour.

ENTRUSTING THEM ALL 221

Give me grace, O God, to pray now with pure and sincere desire for all those with whom I have had to do this day. Let me remember now my friends with love and my enemies with forgiveness, entrusting them all, as I now entrust my own soul and body, to thy protecting care; through Jesus Christ.

MORE FRUIT

222   BEFORE PRAYER

By thy great love draw me, dear Lord, to live much with thee in thought and prayer. Form in me, I pray thee, an abiding habit of laying open all the contents of my heart to thee, so that I refer all my actions to thy will, confiding all my troubles to thy care, all my difficulties to thy guidance, ever seeking with a single mind and all my power to do thy will.

BIBLE READING   *John* 15:1–5

I am the vine, you are the branches. He who abides in me, and I in him, he it is that bears much fruit, for apart from me you can do nothing.

Meditation: Just as the branches are fed by the sap which comes from the root and main stem of a vine, so we draw our life from Christ. Cut off from him we have no life; linked with him we can bear good fruit. Our morning and evening prayer keep us united to him.

SILENCE

Prayer: Root and stem, bough, twig and leaf, 223
the growing tree and the flower of
fruit are one—
one life indivisible, inter-
dependent.
Without thee, we can do nothing;
by thee only bear fruit—much fruit,
and abide in thy love.

FOR OUR FELLOW MEN 224

O God, who hast bound us together in this bundle
of life, give us grace to understand how our lives
depend upon the courage, the industry, the honesty, and the integrity of our fellow men; that we
may be mindful of their needs, grateful for their
faithfulness, and faithful in our responsibilities to
them; through Jesus Christ our Lord.

FRUIT TO LIFE ETERNAL 225

O God, whose hands formed and whose breath
inspires us, let our thoughts go forth with such
good seed of truth, that in the great harvest-home
we may come before thee with joy, bringing our
sheaves with us.

TO REMEMBER TODAY 226

All my fresh springs shall be in thee.

227 OUR RESPONSE TO CHRIST

*What reward shall I give unto the Lord: for all the
benefits that he hath done unto me?*

*I will receive the cup of salvation: and call upon the
Name of the Lord.*

*I will pay my vows now in the presence of all his people:
right dear in the sight of the Lord is the death of his
saints.*

*I will offer to thee the sacrifice of thanksgiving: and will
call upon the Name of the Lord.*

*I will pay my vows unto the Lord, in the sight of all his
people: in the courts of the Lord's house, even in the
midst of thee, O Jerusalem. Praise the Lord.*

228 SIN FORGIVEN

O God, thou hast forgiven me much and my heart
warms with love. Thou hast accepted me who am
altogether unacceptable. When I could not come
to thee, thou didst come to me. O ever-forgiving
God, my heart knows its certainty of forgiveness,
and the fire of love begins to burn. I will heap on it
coals of gratitude for sin forgiven—much sin,
until it blazes with love—much love—for thee,
my God.

229 PRAYER FOR UNITY

O God, the Father of our Lord Jesus Christ, our
only Saviour, the prince of peace: Give us grace
seriously to lay to heart the great dangers we are in
by our unhappy divisions. Take away all hatred
and prejudice, and whatsoever else may hinder us

from godly union and concord: that, as there is but one body, and one Spirit, and one hope of our calling, one Lord, one faith, one baptism, one God, and Father of us all, so we may henceforth be all of one heart, and of one soul, united in one holy bond of truth and peace, of faith and charity, and may with one mind and one mouth glorify thee; through Jesus Christ our Lord.

OUR STRENGTH IS FROM THEE 230

O Lord our God, under the shadow of thy wings let us hope. Thou wilt support us, both when little, and even to gray hairs. When our strength is of thee, it is strength; but, when our own, it is feebleness. We return unto thee, O Lord, that from their weariness our souls may rise towards thee, leaning on the things which thou hast created, and passing on to thyself, who hast wonderfully made them; for with thee is refreshment and true strength.

A BLESSING FOR LOVED ONES 231

May the Lord bless you with all good and keep you from all evil; may he give light to your heart with loving wisdom, and be gracious to you with eternal knowledge; may he lift up his loving countenance upon you for eternal peace.

IN OUR STRIDE

232 GOD MY REFUGE

O God, who hast been the refuge of my fathers through many generations, be my refuge today in every time and circumstance of need. Be my guide through all that is dark and doubtful. Be my guard against all that threatens my spirit's welfare. Be my strength in time of testing. Gladden my heart with thy peace; through Jesus Christ my Lord.

BIBLE READING   *John* 11:20–27

I am the resurrection and the life; he who believes in me, though he die, yet shall he live, and whoever lives and believes in me shall never die.

Meditation: Those who have committed themselves to Jesus Christ share his deathless life, so that when physical death comes they will hardly notice it, they will take it in their stride. Death when it comes will not be the end of life or less life, it will be more life, full life, eternal life.

SILENCE

Prayer: O God, the living God, who hast given 233
unto us a living hope by the resurrection
of Jesus Christ from the dead: grant that
we, being risen with him, may seek the
things which are above, and be made
partakers of the life eternal; through the
same Jesus Christ our Lord.

PRAYER OF LOVE 234
O Father of all, we pray to thee for those whom
we love, but see no longer. Grant them thy peace;
let light perpetual shine upon them; and in thy
loving wisdom and almighty power work in them
the good purpose of thy perfect will; through
Jesus Christ our Lord.

OUR DAILY WORK 235
Remember, O Lord, what thou hast wrought in
us, and not what we deserve; and as thou hast
called us to thy service, make us worthy of our
calling; through Jesus Christ our Lord.

TO REMEMBER TODAY 236
If we live, we live to the Lord, or if we die, we die
to the Lord; so then, whether we live or whether
we die, we are the Lord's.

237 A PSALM OF TRUST

The Lord is my shepherd: therefore can I lack nothing.

He shall feed me in a green pasture: and lead me forth beside the waters of comfort.

He shall convert my soul: and bring me forth in the paths of righteousness, for his Name's sake.

Yea, though I walk through the valley of the shadow of death, I will fear no evil: for thou art with me; thy rod and thy staff comfort me.

Thou shalt prepare a table before me against them that trouble me: thou hast anointed my head with oil, and my cup shall be full.

But thy lovingkindness and mercy shall follow me all the days of my life: and I will dwell in the house of the Lord for ever.

238 FOR HIS SAKE

O God, Spirit of purity and grace, in asking thy forgiveness, I cannot claim a right to be forgiven but only cast myself upon thine unbounded love. I can plead no merit or desert: I can plead no extenuating circumstance: I cannot plead the frailty of my nature: I cannot plead the force of the temptations I encounter: I cannot plead the persuasions of others who led me astray: I can only say, For the sake of Jesus Christ thy Son my Lord.

I believe, O most holy Jesus, that thy saints here below have communion with thy saints above, they praying for us in heaven, we here on earth celebrating their memorials, rejoicing at their bliss, giving thee thanks for their labours of love, and imitating their examples; for which all love, all glory be to thee.

FOR THE DYING 240

O Lord Jesus Christ, who in thy last agony didst commend thy Spirit into the hands of thy heavenly Father, have mercy upon all sick and dying persons; may death be unto them the gate of everlasting life. Grant them at the last the assurance that whether we wake or sleep we are still with thee, who livest and reignest with the Father and the Holy Spirit, one God, for evermore.

PREPARE MY SOUL 241

O thou that hast prepared a place for my soul, prepare my soul for that place; prepare it with holiness; prepare it with desire; and even while it sojourneth upon earth, let it dwell in heaven with thee; beholding the beauty of thy countenance and the glory of thy saints, now and for evermore.

A LAST PRAYER 242

The Lord Almighty grant us a quiet night and a perfect end.

THE PRICE OF HARVEST

243 DEDICATION
O Lord Jesus Christ, who hast created and
redeemed me, and hast brought me unto that
which now I am, thou knowest what thou wouldest do with me; do with me according to thy will;
for thy tender mercy's sake.

BIBLE READING   *John* 12:20–32
Truly, truly, I say to you, unless a grain of wheat
falls into the earth and dies, it remains alone; but if
it dies, it bears much fruit ... and I, when I am
lifted up from the earth, will draw all men to
myself.

> *Meditation: Without the death of the seed there can be
> no crop, without the death of Christ there can be no
> harvest of souls. It is God's love shown in the cross of
> Jesus that has drawn men to him all down the ages.
> The cross proclaims that there is no limit to God's
> love for men.*

SILENCE

Worship: Worthy is the Lamb who was slain, to 244
receive power and wealth and wisdom and
might and honour and glory and blessing! To
him who sits upon the throne and to the Lamb
be blessing and honour and glory and might for
ever and ever!

EACH FOR ALL 245
O God, the king of righteousness, lead us, we pray
thee, in the ways of justice and of peace: inspire us
to break down all tyranny and oppression, to gain
for every man his due reward and from every man
his due service; that each may live for all, and all
may care for each, in the name of Jesus Christ.

FOR THE HUNGRY 246
O merciful and loving Father of all, look down we
pray thee on the many millions who are hungry in
the world today and are at the mercy of disease.
Grant that we who have lived so comfortably and
gently all our lives may have true sympathy with
them and do all in our power, as individuals and as
a nation, to help them to that abundant life which
is thy will for them; through Jesus Christ our
Lord.

TO REMEMBER TODAY 247
God so loved the world that he gave his only Son,
that whoever believes in him should not perish
but have eternal life.

248 THANKSGIVING FOR THE CROSS

Blessed be thy Name, O Jesu, Son of the most high God; Blessed be the sorrow thou sufferedst when thy holy hands and feet were nailed to the tree; and blessed thy love when, the fulness of pain accomplished, thou didst give thy soul into the hands of the Father; so by thy precious cross and precious blood redeeming all the world, all longing souls departed and the numberless unborn; who now livest and reignest in the glory of the eternal Trinity for ever and ever.

249 CONFESSION BEFORE THE CROSS

O God the Father, holy and mighty, who didst give thine only Son to be a sacrifice for us; all we like sheep have gone astray; we have turned every one to his own way; and thou hast laid on him the iniquity of us all. Look mercifully upon us, we beseech thee, as before his cross we meditate and pray; give us faith so to behold him in the mystery of his passion, that we may enter into the fellowship of his sufferings. Let his wounds be our healing, his cross our redemption, and his death our life; through the same Jesus Christ our Lord.

250 FOR THE CHURCH

Almighty God, we beseech thee graciously to behold this thy family, for which our Lord Jesus Christ was contented to be betrayed, and given up into the hands of wicked men, and to suffer death upon the cross, who now liveth and reigneth with thee and the Holy Spirit, ever one God, world without end.

CREATIVE SUFFERING

CREATIVE SUFFERING 251

O Almighty and everlasting God, we praise thee
for teaching us through the cross and resurrection
of thy Son that suffering can be a creative force.
Grant, we pray thee, that as his humiliation won
glory and life, so the sufferings and endurance of
those who follow him may be used to bring his
presence and his power into a needy world,
through the same Jesus Christ our Lord.

COMMENDATION 252

I commend unto thee, O Lord, my soul and my
body, my mind and my thoughts, my vows and
my prayers, my senses and my members, my
words and my deeds, my life and my death, my
loved ones and my friends, my fellow workers
and my assistants; all who need thy help this night,
all Christian folk and all who know thee not.
Enfold us all in thy peace and love, this night and
evermore.

A LAST PRAYER 253

*O Saviour of the world, who by thy cross and precious
blood hast redeemed us: save us and help us, we humbly
beseech thee, O Lord.*

LET MISSION BEGIN

254 READINESS FOR GOD'S WILL

Send out thy light and thy truth, that I may live always near to thee, my God. Let me feel thy love, that I may be—as it were—already in heaven, that I may do all my work as the angels do theirs; and let me be ready for every work, be ready to go out or go in, to stay or depart, just as thou shalt appoint. Lord, let me have no will of my own, or consider my true happiness as depending in the smallest degree on anything that can befall me outwardly, but as consisting altogether in conformity to thy will.

BIBLE READING *John* 20:19–23

"As the Father has sent me, even so I send you." And when he had said this, he breathed on them, and said to them, "Receive the Holy Spirit. If you forgive the sins of any, they are forgiven; if you retain the sins of any, they are retained."

Meditation: Once Christ has been lifted up on the cross the world mission can begin. On the evening of the day of resurrection, the risen Lord sends his disciples forth with the gospel of forgiveness. He knows that they will have hardships and difficulties to face, so he breathes into them his own victorious Spirit.

Thanksgiving: O God, mighty to save, infinite **255**
in compassion towards the nations that know
thee not, and the tongues which cannot speak
thy name: We humbly thank thee that thou hast
made the church of thy dear Son the chariot of
the gospel, to tell it out among the nations that
thou art king, and to bear thy love unto the
world's end: and for all thy servants who
counted not their lives dear unto them on this
employment, and for all peoples newly praising
thee, we praise and bless thee, Father, Son, and
Holy Spirit, one Lord and God for ever.

OUR HIGH CALLING **256**

Into thy hands, O Lord, we commend ourselves
and all who are dear to us this day. Be with us in
our going out and in our coming in. Strengthen us
for the work which thou hast given us to do. And
grant that, filled with thy Holy Spirit, we may
walk worthy of our high calling, and cheerfully
accomplish those things that thou wouldest have
done; through Jesus Christ our Lord.

TO REMEMBER TODAY **257**

You shall be my witnesses to the end of the earth.

258 PRAISE FOR THE GOSPEL

*Praise be to thy Name for the first disciples who were
    sent forth to proclaim the coming of thy kingdom;
for the apostles who, in obedience to thy word, carried
    the gospel to many lands;
for the messengers, known and unknown, who brought
    the good tidings to our own shores
and for all who have gone to the ends of the world with
    the joyful news.
Praise be to thee.*

259 ALL OUR SINS

O Lord Jesus, Son of the living God, grant us of
thy tender grace true fellowship with thee in thy
sufferings, by abhorring and renouncing the open
sins and the secret sins, the habitual sins and the
sudden sins, the little sins and the great sins, which
crucify thee afresh; who now livest and reignest
with the Father and the Holy Spirit, God, for ever
and ever.

260 RISEN POWER FOR THE CHURCH

O Christ, our Lord, whose resurrection did turn
thy timid disciples into men of courage and dar-
ing: Let thy risen power come upon thy church
that she may be bold to proclaim thy saving prin-
ciples to the world. Grant her such a love of the
souls of men that she may draw all men into thy
family and so into union with thee, who with the
Father and the Holy Spirit art our God for ever
and ever.

O Lord and Master Jesus Christ, Word of the
everlasting Father, who hast borne our griefs and
carried the burden of our infirmities; renew by thy
Holy Spirit in thy church, we beseech thee, thy
gifts of healing, and send forth thy disciples again
to preach the gospel of thy kingdom, and to cure
the sick and relieve thy suffering children, to the
praise and glory of thy holy name.

LOVE FOR LOVE   262

Grant, O Lord, that thine unimaginable love
    may find in me some love to meet it.
Let me love the love that ever loves me.
Let my soul's delight be ever to love thee
    and what thou lovest,
    and whom thou lovest,
        as thou lovest,
    now and always, life without end.

A LAST PRAYER   263

*May all the nations whom thou hast made come and
worship thee, O Lord, and glorify thy name.*

THE WAY TO GOD

264 THINGS ETERNAL
My God, I believe in thee: increase my faith. I hope in thee: strengthen my hope. I love thee, and desire to love thee more and more, and above all things, and all others for thee: quicken my love and make me wholly thine.

BIBLE READING *Hebrews 4:14–16*
For we have not a high priest who is unable to sympathize with our weaknesses, but one who in every respect has been tempted as we are, yet without sinning.

Meditation: Jesus, the ascended Lord and universal high priest, leads us into the presence of God. He knows what it is to be man, for he has lived as man, and has resisted evil unto death. We can share his victorious life and follow him to the throne of God's grace and glory.

SILENCE

Prayer: Daily in spirit, in thy Holy Spirit,
let me behold thee on the throne of
God,
thou king reigning in holiness,
thou conqueror of all evil,
thou majesty of love,
very God and very man,
of glory unimaginable and eternal,
in whom all hope is sure.

THE COUNTLESS MILLIONS

O glorious Christ, who in thy ascension didst enter into thy kingdom: Remember, we pray thee, the countless millions who have not heard of the redemption which thou hast won for them. Grant that they may learn, through thy church, of the new and living way which thou hast opened for them. Let them draw near in fulness of faith, to enter with thee into the holy place of the Father's presence, and receive forgiveness and peace. So may they worship, with the innumerable company of angels and with the spirits of just men made perfect, Father, Son and Holy Spirit, one God, blessed for evermore.

TO REMEMBER TODAY

If then you have been raised with Christ, seek the things that are above, where Christ is, seated at the right hand of God.

268 PRAISE TO THE ASCENDED CHRIST
Thou art the King of glory: O Christ.
Thou art the everlasting Son: of the Father.
When thou tookest upon thee to deliver man:
   Thou didst not abhor the Virgin's womb.
When thou hadst overcome the sharpness of death:
   thou didst open the kingdom of heaven to all
      believers.
Thou sittest at the right hand of God:
   in the glory of the Father.
We believe that thou shalt come:
   to be our Judge.

269 IN THY SIGHT
Lord, help us to know ourselves as we are, to see
ourselves as we are in thy sight, and also in hope to
see ourselves as we shall be, when thou hast
finished thy work in us, through Jesus Christ our
Lord.

270 FOR UNION WITH CHRIST
O Lord Christ, our great high priest, whose prayers and promises were not for thy disciples only,
but for all those who should believe on thee by
their word, unto the world's end: Breathe upon us
thy holy and glorious Spirit, to knit us to thyself
and to one another in an indestructible bond; as
thou and the Father are one in the unity of the
same Spirit, God for ever and ever.

FOR THE DEAF AND DUMB

O God, the Father of our Lord Jesus Christ, who opened the ears of the deaf and made the dumb to speak; bless, we pray thee, all thy deaf children, that through thy grace they may be more than conquerors. Give us such sympathy with them, that spirit may speak to spirit in love and companionship, through the same Jesus Christ our Lord.

FOR THE CHURCH

We beseech thee, O Lord, to guide thy church with thy perpetual governance that it may walk warily in times of quiet, and boldly in times of trouble, through Jesus Christ our Lord.

A LAST PRAYER

Now the God of peace, that brought again from the dead our Lord Jesus, that great shepherd of the sheep, through the blood of the everlasting covenant, make us perfect in every good work to do his will, working in us that which is well-pleasing in his sight, through Jesus Christ; to whom be glory for ever and ever.

THE DIRECT RESULT

274   BEFORE BIBLE STUDY

Lord of the harvest, who dost sow good seed into the hearts of all men: Grant that our hearts may not be so hardened by the world's traffic that the seed can take no root; nor so shallow that the roots can find no depth; nor so cumbered with the cares and riches of the world that the growing shoots are choked; but that we may be good ground, bearing good fruit; to the glory of thy name.

BIBLE READING   *Galatians 5:16–24*

The fruit of the Spirit is love, joy, peace, patience, kindness, goodness, faithfulness, gentleness, self-control; against such there is no law. And those who belong to Christ Jesus have crucified the flesh with its passions and desires.

> *Meditation: If we have the Holy Spirit in us, these virtues will follow as a matter of course. We don't have to struggle for each one separately, but let the Spirit of Jesus come into us. Then love, joy, peace and the others will appear naturally, as the grapes come on the vine.*

SILENCE

Prayer: O most Holy Spirit,   275
   possess me by thy peace,
   illuminate me by thy truth,
   fire me by thy flame,
   enable me by thy power,
   be made visible in me by thy fruits,
   lift me by grace upon grace
    from glory to glory,
   O Spirit of the Lord;
  who art with the Father and the Son one
  God,
    world without end.

FOR ALL IN AUTHORITY   276

O Father of the just, do thou of thine infinite
goodness direct the hearts of all who bear authority. Help them with the power of thy Holy Spirit
to make laws in accordance with thy will, and for
the advancement of righteousness. Protect them
from the snares of the enemy and the deceits of the
world; let no pride of power betray them into
rejection of thy commandments; and grant that
both rulers and people may with one mind serve
thee our God and king, through Jesus Christ.

TO REMEMBER TODAY   277

Come, thou Holy Spirit, come!

278 THE WAY OF GOD'S COMMANDMENTS

> *Teach me, O Lord, the way of thy statutes:*
> * and I shall keep it unto the end.*
> *Give me understanding, and I shall keep thy law:*
> * yea, I shall keep it with my whole heart.*
> *Make me to go in the path of thy commandments:*
> * for therein is my desire.*
> *Incline my heart unto thy testimonies:*
> * and not to covetousness.*
> *O turn away mine eyes, lest they behold vanity:*
> * and quicken thou me in thy way.*
> *Behold, my delight is in thy commandments:*
> * O quicken me in thy righteousness.*

279 FOR FORGIVENESS

Almighty God, who hast pity on our weakness, we humbly confess to thee the many faults and failures of the work we have done in thy name, asking thee to forgive us that which is past and to give us thy help and guidance that we may serve thee more faithfully in the time to come, through Jesus Christ our Lord.

280 INTO THY HAND

Into thy hands, our Father, we commit this thy world, this thy family, for which our Lord Jesus Christ was content to be betrayed, and to suffer death upon the cross. Into thy hands we commit thy universal church and her unity. Into thy hands we commit all the problems which seem insoluble, in sure and certain hope; for in thee is our trust. Here and now, we lay all in thy hands. All love, all glory, be unto thee, for ever and ever.

LET GRACE PREVAIL 281

Lord, I do not presume to tell thee what to do, or how or when to do it, I simply bring before thee people who need thy love and needs which thy grace alone can meet. Let love reign, O Lord my God, let grace prevail.

FOR TEACHERS AND STUDENTS 282

Grant, O Lord, to all teachers and students, to love that which is worth loving, to know that which is worth knowing, to praise that which pleaseth thee most, to esteem that which is most precious unto thee, and to dislike whatsoever is evil in thine eyes. Grant us with true judgment to distinguish things that differ, and above all, to search out and to do what is well-pleasing unto thee; through Jesus Christ our Lord.

A LAST PRAYER 283

Defend, O Lord, me thy child with thy heavenly grace, that I may continue thine for ever; and daily increase in thy Holy Spirit, more and more, until I come unto thy everlasting kingdom. Amen.

DEAD UNLESS I DIE

284 FOR CHRIST-LIKENESS
O Lord Jesus Christ, who didst deign to be made
like unto men: the sharer of our sorrows, the
companion of our journeys, the light of our ignor-
ance, the remedy of our infirmity: So fill us with
thy Spirit and endue us with thy grace that as thou
hast been made like unto us, we may grow more
like unto thee, for thy tender mercies' sake.

BIBLE READING   *Galatians* 2:20
I have been crucified with Christ; it is no longer I
who live, but Christ who lives in me; and the life I
now live in the flesh I live by faith in the Son of
God, who loved me and gave himself for me.

> *Meditation: If Christ is to live in me, my lower self
> must die. All lust and greed, all wanting my own
> way, all seeking my own interest, all pushing myself
> forward, all envy and jealousy of others must go.
> This is a painful business, like crucifixion. I shall be
> spiritually dead as long as I refuse to die.*

SILENCE

Prayer: O merciful God, grant that the old 285 Adam in this child may be so buried that the new man may be raised up in me. Grant that all evil desires of the flesh may die in me, and that all things belonging to the Spirit may live and grow in me.

FOLLOWING CHRIST 286
Almighty God, who hast shown in the life and teaching of thy Son the true way of blessedness, thou hast also showed us in his suffering and death that the path of love may lead to the cross, and the reward of faithfulness may be a crown of thorns. Give us grace to learn these hard lessons. May we take up our cross and follow Christ in the strength of patience and the constancy of faith; and may we have such fellowship with him in his sorrow that we may know the secret of his strength and peace, and see even in our darkest hour the shining of the eternal light, for his sake who died and rose again for us, the same Jesus Christ our Lord.

FOR TODAY 287
Teach us, good Lord, to serve thee as thou deservest; to give and not to count the cost; to fight and not to heed the wounds; to toil and not to seek for rest; to labour and to ask for no reward, save that of knowing that we do thy will; through Jesus Christ our Lord.

TO REMEMBER TODAY 288
If any one is in Christ, he is a new creation; the old has passed away, behold, the new has come.

289 THANKSGIVING

The Lord is full of compassion and mercy:
longsuffering, and of great goodness.
He will not always be chiding:
neither keepeth he his anger for ever.
He hath not dealt with us after our sins:
nor rewarded us according to our wickednesses.
For look how high the heaven is in comparison of the
earth:
so great is his mercy also toward them that fear him.
Look how wide also the east is from the west:
so far hath he set our sins from us.
Yea, like as a father pitieth his own children:
even so is the Lord merciful unto them that fear him.

290 DEATH TO SIN

O God our Father, help us to nail to the cross of thy dear Son the whole body of our death, the wrong desires of the heart, the sinful devisings of the mind, the corrupt apprehensions of the eyes, the cruel words of the tongue, the ill employment of hands and feet; that the old man being crucified and done away, the new man may live and grow into the glorious likeness of the same thy Son Jesus Christ; who liveth and reigneth with thee and the Holy Spirit, one God, world without end.

FOR THE CHURCHES

O thou who walkest in the midst of the churches and knowest their works, cleanse and renew thy churches today, that by their witness the nations of the world may be gathered unto thee, who livest and reignest with the Father and the Holy Spirit, one God for ever and ever.

STRENGTHEN MY BACK

Lord, teach me the art of patience whilst I am well, and give me the use of it when I am sick. In that day either lighten my burden or strengthen my back. Make me, who so often in my health have discovered my weakness, presuming on my own strength, to be strong in my sickness when I solely rely on thy assistance. Through Jesus Christ my Lord.

DEDICATION

Take, Lord, all my liberty. Receive my memory, my understanding and my whole will. Whatever I have and possess thou hast given to me; to thee I restore it wholly, and to thy will I utterly surrender it for thy direction. Give me the love of thee only, with thy grace, and I am rich enough; nor ask I anything beside.

A LAST THOUGHT

When I wake up after thy likeness, I shall be satisfied with it.

BIRTH PANGS

295 FOR RENEWAL
O Almighty God, who sittest upon the throne,
make all things within us new this day. Renew our
faith, and hope, and love; renew our wills, that we
may serve thee gladly and watchfully with all our
powers; renew our delight in thy truth and in thy
worship; renew our joy in thee, our longing that
all may know thee, our desires and labours to
serve others. And so take care of us thy people,
who embrace the cross of thy Son and desire to
walk in the light and power of thy Spirit, now and
evermore.

BIBLE READING   *Romans* 8:18–22
We know that the whole creation has been groan-
ing in travail together until now ... For the
creation waits with eager longing for the revealing
of the sons of god.

> *Meditation: St. Paul suggests that God's new*
> *creation is waiting for God's new man. The creation*
> *of the universe according to God's will waits till the*
> *creation of man is finished. God calls all who have*
> *been made new in Christ Jesus to be fellow workers in*
> *completing the new world.*

Prayer: O Lord Christ, who art the head of the 296
redeemed humanity, in whom all may find forgiveness, love and brotherhood, we come to
thee in gratitude and trust because thou hast
taken us into thy new creation. Help us to
rejoice in the fellowship of the redeemed, seeing
in our fellow Christians those who have been
re-born in thee; and in all who know thee not,
those whom thou didst die to save and whom
thou wouldest call to be our brethren. Glory to
thee, O blessed Saviour, now and through all
ages.

FOR THOSE WE LOVE   297

O thou who hast ordered this wondrous world,
who knowest all things in earth and heaven, so fill
our hearts with trust in thee, that by night and by
day, at all times and in all seasons, we may without
fear commit those who are dear to us to thy
never-failing love, for this life and the life to come.

TO REMEMBER TODAY   298

I am the Alpha and the Omega, says the Lord God,
who is and who was and is to come, the Almighty.

299 A CALL TO PRAISE

O be joyful in the Lord, all ye lands:
  serve the Lord with gladness, and come before his
    presence with a song.
Be ye sure that the Lord he is God:
  it is he that hath made us, and not we ourselves; we
    are his people, and the sheep of his pasture.
O go your way into his gates with thanksgiving, and
    into his courts with praise:
  be thankful unto him, and speak good of his name.
For the Lord is gracious, his mercy is everlasting:
  and his truth endureth from generation to generation.

300 PENITENCE

Almighty and everlasting God, who hatest
nothing that thou hast made, and dost forgive the
sins of all them that are penitent: Create and make
in us new and contrite hearts, that we worthily
lamenting our sins, and acknowledging our
wretchedness, may obtain of thee, the God of all
mercy, perfect remission and forgiveness;
through Jesus Christ our Lord.

301 SIGNS OF THE KINGDOM

O God, we pray thee for thy church which is set
today amid the perplexities of a changing order,
and is face to face with a new task: Fill us afresh
with the Spirit of Pentecost; help us to bear witness boldly to the coming of thy kingdom; and do
thou hasten the time when the knowledge of thyself shall fill the earth, as the waters cover the sea.

THE HEAVY LADEN

O blessed Jesus Christ, who didst bid all who carry heavy burdens to come to thee, refresh us with thy presence and thy power. Quicken our understanding and give ease to our hearts by bringing us close to things infinite and eternal. Open to us the mind of God, that in his light we may see light. And crown thy choice of us to be thy servants, by making us springs of strength and joy to all whom we serve.

THE ETERNAL CHANGELESSNESS

Be present, O merciful God, and protect us through the silent hours of this night, so that we who are wearied by the changes and chances of this fleeting world, may repose upon thy eternal changelessness; through Jesus Christ our Lord.

A LAST THOUGHT

This God is our God for ever and ever: he shall be our guide unto death—and beyond.

COMPLETING CREATION

305 A MORNING PRAYER

Into thy hands, O heavenly Father, I commit myself, body and soul. Let thy holy angel be with me, that the evil one may have no power over me. Help and bless thy church; hold thy protecting hand over this land and people; have pity upon those who are in distress and need. O God, let the light of thy truth shine upon us, and bring us at last to thy heavenly kingdom; through Jesus Christ our Lord.

BIBLE READING   *Ephesians* 1:3–10

For he has made known to us in all wisdom and insight the mystery of his will, according to his purpose which he set forth in Christ as a plan for the fulness of time, to unite all things in him, things in heaven and things on earth.

Meditation: Here is God's eternal purpose made clear—to gather everything into Christ Jesus, all men and all truth, the whole universe. The task of the church is to bring every man into Christ, to redeem every human activity, so that the eternal Christ may be complete. Then our triumphant Lord will offer the completed kingdom to the Father.

Praise: Blessed be thou, O God,   **306**
    who hast declared that it is thine eternal
        purpose to gather in one all things
        in Christ.
    Worthy art thou to receive honour and
        power and glory,
    for the great love wherewith thou hast
        loved all mankind,
      and hast delivered us from the powers
        of darkness,
      and brought us into the kingdom of
        thy Son.

FOR STAYING POWER   **307**

O Lord God, when thou givest to thy servants to endeavour any great matter, grant us also to know that it is not the beginning, but the continuing of the same unto the end, until it be throughly finished, which yieldeth the true glory; through him who for the finishing of thy work laid down his life, our redeemer, Jesus Christ.

TO REMEMBER TODAY   **308**

For from him and through him and to him are all things. To him be glory for ever. Amen.

309 WORSHIP

> O praise God in his holiness:
> praise him in the firmament of his power.
> Praise him in his noble acts:
> praise him according to his excellent greatness.
> Praise him in the sound of the trumpet:
> praise him upon the lute and harp.
> Praise him in the cymbals and dances:
> praise him upon the strings and pipe.
> Praise him upon the well-tuned cymbals:
> praise him upon the loud cymbals.
> Let every thing that hath breath:
> praise the Lord.

310 RETURN TO GOD

O Lord, after I have journeyed through the years, through the months (not less at the end of each single day), let me return unto the one beginning. In all perplexity of mind, vexation of heart, weariness of spirit, after failure and sin—make me return to the one beginning, that I may begin again, my Father, my Saviour, my life, my glory.

311 THE WORK OF MAN'S SALVATION

O God of unchangeable power and eternal light, look favourably on thy whole church, that wonderful and sacred mystery; and by the tranquil operation of thy perpetual providence, carry out the work of man's salvation; and let the whole world feel and see that things which were cast down are being raised up, and things which had grown old are being made new, and all things are returning to perfection through him from whom they took their origin, even through our Lord Jesus Christ.

EVENING TIME   312
Abide with us, O Lord, for it is toward evening and the day is far spent: abide with us, and with thy whole church. Abide with us in the evening of the day, in the evening of life, in the evening of the world. Abide with us and with all thy faithful ones, O Lord, in time and eternity.

PRAYER FOR ALL   313
The blessing of the Lord rest and remain upon all his people, in every land, of every tongue; the Lord meet in mercy all that seek him; the Lord comfort all who suffer and mourn; the Lord hasten his coming, and give us, his people, the blessing of peace.

A LAST PRAYER   314
Grant, O Lord Christ, that I may be present on that day when thou shalt offer the completed universe to thy Father, and he shall be all in all.

THE DIVINE VISITOR

315 ADORATION

O God, who requirest that we should seek thee
and makest us to find thee, and openest to us when
we knock: O God, from whom to be averted is to
fall, and to whom to be turned is to rise; in whom
to abide is to be established: O God, whom to
know is to live, whom to serve is to reign; I praise
thee, I bless thee, I adore thee, my God.

BIBLE READING   *Revelation* 3:20

Behold, I stand at the door and knock; if any one
hears my voice and opens the door, I will come in
to him and eat with him, and he with me.

*Meditation: Jesus comes from God to awaken the
spirit of man created in God's image. That God-
created nature in man is often so overlaid that it gets
no chance to grow, so masked by the lower self that it
is seldom seen. But it is still there, and our Lord
knocks . . . and calls . . . and waits . . . and listens.
One day the prisoner who is shut within, will hear
the quiet, persistent knocking, and will let the Lord
in.*

Prayer: Come, Lord Jesus, and live in the souls **316** of us thy servants. Come in the fulness of thy purity and thy power, in the holiness of thy Spirit, in the perfection of thy mysteries, and overcome all adverse powers in thy Spirit, to the glory of God the Father.

MASTER OF THE HOUSE 317

Be present with us, O Lord, in our daily duties, and grant to those who dwell in this house the strength and protection of thy continual help; that thou mayest be known as the Master of the family and the defender of this home; through Jesus Christ our Lord.

FOR AN OPEN HEART 318

O Lord, of thy tender love open my whole heart to receive thee; let nothing shut thee out, nothing be shut to thee. Thou alone canst fit my heart for thyself; cleanse it wholly by thy Spirit, that it may wholly love thee; be wholly filled with thee; wholly penetrated, enlightened, warmed by thee; that thou mayest dwell in it for ever, and it may love thee with thine own love in it everlastingly.

TO REMEMBER TODAY 319

Today salvation has come to this house.

320　EVENING PRAISE

O Lord our Governor, how excellent is thy name in all
the world: thou that hast set thy glory above the
heavens!

For I will consider thy heavens, even the works of thy
fingers: the moon and the stars, which thou hast
ordained.

What is man, that thou art mindful of him: and the son
of man, that thou visitest him?

Thou madest him lower than the angels: to crown him
with glory and worship.

Thou madest him to have dominion over the works of
thy hands: and thou hast put all things in subjection
under his feet.

O Lord our Governor: how excellent is thy name in all
the world!

321　A SINFUL MAN, O LORD

O Holy Lord, in the holiness of thy presence all
my sinful nature cries out "Depart". Yet if thou
take me at my word I am indeed lost and forsaken.
Come then, O Lord of holiness, heavenly guest,
enter now and cleanse the house of my soul and
abide with me for ever.

322　FIRE ON THE EARTH

Almighty God, whose Son Jesus Christ came to
cast fire upon the earth: Grant that by the prayers
of thy faithful people a fire of burning zeal may be
kindled and pass from heart to heart, that the light

of thy church may shine forth bright and clear to all mankind; through the same thy Son Jesus Christ our Lord.

AS WE GROW OLD 323

O Lord Jesus Christ, who didst hearken unto the prayer of thy two disciples and abide with them, when it was toward evening and the day was far spent: Abide, we pray thee, with thine aged servants in the evening of life. Make thyself known unto them, and whensoever they shall pass through the valley of the shadow of death, be thou with them and bring them safe to their eternal home.

THREE COMINGS 324

Let me love thee, O Christ, in thy first coming, when thou wast made man, for love of man, and for love of me. Let me love thee, O Christ, in thy second coming, when with inconceivable love, thou standest and knockest at the door, and wouldest enter into the souls of men, and into mine. Plant in my soul, O Christ, thy likeness of love; that when by death thou callest, it may be ready, and burning, to come unto thee.

A LAST THOUGHT 325

The eternal God is your dwelling place, and underneath are the everlasting arms.

LITANIES

A LITANY OF FAITH

326 Jesus said: All things are possible to him who believes.
Lord, I believe, help thou mine unbelief.

Jesus said: Do not be anxious about tomorrow; your heavenly Father knows that you need all these things.
Lord, I believe, help thou mine unbelief.

Jesus said: Thy faith hath saved thee, go in peace.
Lord, I believe, help thou mine unbelief.

Jesus said: Your heavenly Father will give the Holy Spirit to them that ask him.
Lord, I believe, help thou mine unbelief.

Jesus appeared unto the twelve and upbraided them for their unbelief.
Lord, I believe, help thou mine unbelief.

Jesus said: Blessed are those who have not seen but yet believed.
Lord, I believe, help thou mine unbelief.

Jesus said: Let down your nets for a draught.
Master, we have toiled all night and taken nothing, but at thy word I will let down the net.

Jesus said: Lo, I am with you always, even unto the end of the world.
Lord, I believe, help thou mine unbelief.

A LITANY OF THE INDWELLING CHRIST

O Christ, thou art the spring of living water, 327
O Christ, thou art the bread of life,
O Christ, thou art the vine,

O Christ, thou art in us, and we in thee and in the Father.

O Christ, thy God is our God,
O Christ, thy Father is our Father,
O Christ, thy brethren are our brethren,

O Christ, thou art in us, and we in thee and in the Father.

O Christ, the risen one,
O Christ, the conqueror,
O Christ, the living one,

O Christ, thou art in us, and we in thee and in the Father.

O Christ, thou art in us, and we in thee and in the Father.

O Christ, the dayspring from on high,
O Christ, the light of the world,
O Christ, reflection of the Father's glory,

O Christ, thou art in us, and we in thee and in the Father.

A LITANY OF DAILY TRUST

328 Lord, thou hast always given me bread for
tomorrow:
>> But today I am poor,
>> Lord, I believe.

Lord, thou hast always given me strength for
tomorrow:
>> But today I am feeble,
>> Lord, I believe.

Lord, thou hast always given me peace for
tomorrow:
>> But today I am anxious,
>> Lord, I believe.

Lord, thou hast always traced for me the way:
>> But today, the way is hidden,
>> Lord, I believe.

Lord, thou hast always spoken to me at the right
moment:
>> And in spite of thy silence today,
>> Lord, I believe.

Lord, thou hast always been a faithful friend:
>> And in spite of those who betray,
>> Today, I believe.

Lord, thou hast always fulfilled thy promises:
>> And in spite of those who doubt,
>> Today, I believe.

A LITANY OF PRAYER WITH CHRIST

Holy Father, keep them in thy name whom thou 329 hast given me.
  Amen. Holy Father, keep us in thy name.

Holy Father, keep them from the evil one.
  Amen. Holy Father, keep us from the evil one.

Holy Father, sanctify them in thy truth.
  Amen. Holy Father, sanctify us in thy truth.

Holy Father, grant that they may all be one.
  Amen. Holy Father, make us one.

Holy Father, grant that they may have my joy.
  Amen. Holy Father, give us his joy.

Holy Father, grant that they may be in us.
  Amen. Holy Father, as thou art in him, and he in thee.

Holy Father, grant that they may behold my glory.
  Amen. Holy Father, show us his glory.

Holy Father, grant that thy love may be in them.
  Amen. Holy Father, let thy love be in us.

So that the world may believe that thou hast sent me.
  Amen. Holy Father, let the world believe.

SOURCES OF PRAYERS

The compiler and publishers express their thanks to the authors and publishers who have given permission for prayers to be included in this book. They have made every effort to trace the copyright of all the prayers quoted; if there has been any inadvertent infringement, they will gladly make suitable acknowledgment in subsequent editions. Full details are given in each case under the first reference.

The Bible Reading for each morning is taken from the Revised Standard Version. For the other quotations from the Bible, the Authorized Version or the Revised Standard Version or the Prayer Book Version has been used.

1. *Sursum Corda* (Mowbray)
2. *New Every Morning* (British Broadcasting Corporation)
3. Bishop Walsham How
4. Archbishop William Temple, 1881–1944
5. Psalm 104:33
6. Liturgy of S. James
7. G.A. (George Appleton)
8. G.A.
9. Percy Dearmer, 1867–1936
10. Bishop B. F. Westcott, 1825–1901
11. Psalm 4:9
12. Gelasian Sacramentary
13. G.A.
14. *A Diary of Private Prayer,* John Baillie (Oxford University Press)
15. Père Grou, 1731–1803
16. Jeremiah 31:3
17. Ephesians 3:14–19
18. G.A.
19. G.A.
20. United Society for the Propagation of the Gospel, London
21. S. Augustine, 354–430
22. Psalm 31:6
23. *My God my Glory*, E. Milner-White (S.P.C.K.)
24. *Meditations and Prayers*, Evelyn Underhill (Longmans, Green & Co. Ltd.)
25. G.A.

94. Alcuin, A.D. 780
95. S. Augustine's College, Canterbury
96. G.A.
97. Mozarabic Liturgy
98. I John 4:16
99. *My God my Glory*
100. Bishop Cosin, 1594–1672
101. *Faith and Order Manual* 1927 (World Council of Churches)
102. John Hunter, 1849–1917
103. Luke 18:13
104. Psalm 51:1–3, 9–11
105. G.A.
106. Jeremy Taylor, 1612–1667
107. R. M. Benson, 1824–1915
108. B.C.P.
109. Luke 7:47
110. S. Augustine
111. *Daily Prayer*
112. *Daily Prayer*
113. *A Diary of Private Prayer*
114. I Samuel 3:9
115. Psalm 46:1–3, 6, 10
116. Dean Vaughan, 1816–1897
117. G.A.
118. *The Book of Common Order* (of the Church of Scotland)
119. G.A.
120. Psalm 18:35
121. Père Grou, 1731–1803
122. *Daily Prayer*
123. S. Paul's Cathedral
124. William Bright, 1824–1901
125. Matthew 9:2
126. Te Deum Laudamus
127. G.A.
128. B.C.P.
129. *Prayers New and Old*
130. *The Book of Common Order*
131. G.A.
132. William Bright, 1824–1901
133. B.C.P.
134. *Student Prayer* (S.C.M. Press)
135. John 17:3
136. Psalm 19:7–12, 14–15
137. B.C.P.
138. Archbishop Laud, 1573–1645
139. G.A.
140. *Sarum Primer* 1558
141. S. Anselm, 1033–1107
142. S. Francis of Assisi, 1182–1226
143. *The Prayer Manual*, F. B. Macnutt (Mowbray)
144. Isaiah 26:3
145. Psalm 122:1–2, 6–9
146. Archbishop William Temple
147. *Prayers New and Old*
148. *The Book of Common Order*
149. *My God my Glory*
150. Untraced
151. Edward Dering (Sixteenth Century)
152. *Daily Prayer*
153. A Book of Prayers for Students (S.C.M. Press)
154. Romans 5:5
155. Ephesians 3:14–19
156. G.A.
157. G.A.
158. G.A.
159. *My God my Glory*
160. John 14:27
161. *Prayers New and Old*

162. *My God my Glory*
163. *Prayers of the World-Wide Church* (U.S.P.G.)
164. *An Anthology of Prayers,* A.S.T. Fisher (Longmans, Green & Co. Ltd.)
165. John 1:18
166. B.C.P.
167. *Daily Prayer*
168. G.A.
169. Mothers' Union
170. Bishop B. F. Westcott, 1825–1901
171. *My God my Glory*
172. B.C.P.
173. Dean Vaughan, 1816–1897
174. Untraced
175. *New Every Morning*
176. Psalm 40:7–8
177. The Benedictus
178. *The Book of Common Order*
179. Ancient
180. G.A.
181. *My God my Glory*
182. Philippians 4:7
183. Cardinal Newman, 1801–1890
184. E. B. Pusey, 1800–1882
185. *A Diary of Private Prayer*
186. Philippians 4:13
187. Psalm 4:1, 5–9
188. *The Book of Common Order*
189. W. E. Orchard
190. *A Diary of Private Prayer*
191. *My God my Glory*
192. 1 Peter 5:7
193. B.C.P.
194. Erasmus, 1466–1536
195. *The Prayer Manual*
196. John 6:68
197. Psalm 36:5–10
198. G.A.
199. G.A.
200. G.A.
201. *My God my Glory*
202. Isaiah 40:31
203. *The Book of Common Order*
204. *My God my Glory*
205. *The Kingdom, the Power and the Glory,* E. Milner-White (O.U.P.)
206. Deuteronomy 8:3
207. Psalm 145:15–19, 21
208. A Sufi Prayer
209. G.A.
210. G.A.
211. *My God my Glory*
212. G.A.
213. *The Book of Common Order*
214. *The World At One In Prayer,* Daniel Johnson Fleming (Harper & Bros., New York)
215. Bishop Crick, *The Prayer Manual*
216. Psalm 43:3
217. Psalm 27:1, 3–5, 7
218. G.A.
219. Peter Green
220. Arthur W. Robinson, *Prayers New and Old* (S.C.M. Press)
221. *A Diary of Private Prayer*
222. Oxford Mission to Calcutta
223. *My God my Glory*
224. Reinhold Niebuhr, *The Prayer Manual*
225. Bishop Henry Sylvester Nash

ACKNOWLEDGMENTS

We desire to acknowledge with gratitude permission by the undermentioned authors, owners of copyright and publishers (as at 1962) to include prayers in this volume (listed above):

The Warden, S. Augustine's College, Canterbury; The Rt. Rev. Leslie Hunter, Bishop of Sheffield; The Archdeacon of Sheffield; The Industrial Christian Fellowship; The Very Rev. E. Milner-White, Dean of York; The Mothers' Union; The Oxford Mission to Calcutta; The Dean and Chapter of S. Paul's Cathedral; The Father Superior, The Society of S. John the Evangelist, for prayers by R. M. Benson; Lady Sykes, for prayers by Dr. Percy Dearmer; Mrs. William Temple.

The British Broadcasting Corporation, *New Every Morning*; Forward Movement Publications, U.S.A., *Prayers New and Old*, *Prayers of Henry Sylvester Nash*; Harper & Brothers, New York, *The World at One in Prayer*; Messrs. Longmans, Green & Co. Ltd., *An Anthology of Prayers, Meditations and Prayers*; Messrs. A. R. Mowbray & Co. Ltd., *After the Third Collect*, *The Prayer Manual*, *Sursum Corda*; Oxford University Press, *A Book of Public Worship*, *A Diary of Private Prayer*, *Daily Prayer*, *The Kingdom*, *The Power and The Glory*; Society for Promoting Christian Knowledge, *A Procession of Passion Prayers*, *My God my Glory*; Society for the Propagation of the Gospel, *Prayers*

INDEX OF SUBJECTS
The references are to the numbers beside
the prayers.

ABOUT THE AUTHOR

George Appleton is a well-known English author and churchman who lives in Oxfordshire. He studied at Selwyn College, Cambridge, and at St. Augustine's College, Canterbury; he became a minister, missionary, and bishop of the Church of England. After serving in English parish churches, he became missionary in charge of the S.P.G. Mission, Irrawaddy Delta. He was Warden of the College of the Holy Cross, Rangoon, and Archdeacon of Rangoon; and after World War II, he was for two years Director of Public Relations for the government of Burma. Upon returning to Great Britain, he again served parish churches, was Secretary of the Conference of British Missionary Societies, and became Archdeacon of London and Canon of St. Paul's Cathedral. He later became Archbishop of Perth, Australia, and then Anglican Archbishop in Jerusalem. He is known around the world for his widely used books of prayers and devotions.